ATHENE
SERIES

GENERAL EDITORS
Gloria Bowles
Renate Klein
Janice Raymond

CONSULTING EDITOR
Dale Spender

The **Athene Series** assumes that those who formulate explanations of the way the world works need to know and appreciate the significance of basic feminist principles.

The growth of feminist research internationally has called into question almost all aspects of social organization in our culture. The **Athene Series** focuses on the construction of knowledge and the exclusion of women from the process—both as theorists and subjects of study—and offers innovative studies that challenge established theories and research.

ATHENE, the Olympian goddess of wisdom, was honored by the ancient Greeks as the patron of arts and sciences and guardian of cities. She represented both peace and war, the latter in its cognitive aspect. Her mother, Metis, was a Titan and presided over all knowledge. While pregnant with Athene, Metis was swallowed whole by Zeus. Some say this was his attempt to embody her supreme wisdom. The original Athene is thus twice born: once of her strong mother, Metis, and once more out of the head of Zeus. According to feminist myth, there is a "third birth" of Athene when she stops being an agent and mouthpiece of Zeus and male dominance, and returns to her original source: the wisdom of womankind.

Crucial Conversations

....

Interpreting Contemporary American Literary Autobiographies by Women

....

Jeanne Braham

ATHENE SERIES

Teachers College Press
Teachers College, Columbia University
New York and London

Published by Teachers College Press,
1234 Amsterdam Avenue, New York, NY 10027

Library of Congress Cataloging-in-Publication Data

Braham, Jeanne
    Crucial conversations : interpreting contemporary American literary autobiographies by women / Jeanne Braham.
        p.   cm. — (Athene series)
    Includes bibliographical references and index.
    ISBN 0-8077-6279-2 — ISBN 0-8077-6278-4 (pbk.)
    1. American prose literature—Women authors—History and criticism.   2. Women authors, American—20th century—Biography—History and criticism.   3. American prose literature—20th century—History and criticism.   4. Women and literature—United States—History—20th century.   5. Autobiography—Women authors.
    6. Authorship—Sex differences.   I. Title.   II. Series.
    PS366.A88B73   1995
    810.9'492072—dc20   94-38417

ISBN 0-8077-6279-2
ISBN 0-8077-6278-4 (pbk.)

Printed on acid-free paper
Manufactured in the United States of America

01 00 99 98 97 96 95   8 7 6 5 4 3 2 1

Grateful acknowledgment is made to the following for permission to reprint the material indicated:

From *In My Mother's House*. Copyright © 1983 by Kim Chernin. Reprinted by permission of Ticknor & Fields/Houghton Mifflin Co. All rights reserved.

London—1944, by Mary Lee Settle. Reprinted from *Virginia Quarterly Review*, volume 63, Autumn 1987, pages 565–586. Reprinted by permission of *Virginia Quarterly Review*.

"Wintering Over," by Maxine Kumin. *Country Living*, September 1978. Stanford, Connecticut, Cowles Magazines, Inc. Reprinted by permission.

"An Interview with Virginia Elson and Beverlee Hughes." *Yes: A Magazine of Poetry* 4, no. 3 (Spring-Summer 1974).

Reprinted by permission of Curtis Brown, Ltd. Copyright 1987, Excerpted from *In Deep* by Maxine Kumin. Used by permission of Curtis Brown Ltd.

Excerpts from *Salvador*, by Joan Didion, 1983. Reprinted by permission of Janklow & Nesbit Associates.

Audre Lorde, selections from *The Cancer Journals*, 1980, Spinsters/Aunt Lute; selections from *Sister Outsider*, 1984, Crossing Press. Reprinted by permission of the Charlotte Sheedy Agency.

From *Daybook: The Journal of an Artist*, by Anne Truitt. Copyright © 1982 by Anne Truitt. Reprinted by permission of Pantheon Books, a division of Random House, Inc.

Excerpts from *Fierce Attachments* by Vivian Gornick. Copyright © 1987 by Vivian Gornick. Reprinted by permission of Farrar, Straus & Giroux, Inc.

From *I Know Why the Caged Bird Sings* by Maya Angelou. Reprinted by permission of Random House, Inc. © 1969.

From *Outrageous Acts and Everyday Rebellions* by Gloria Steinem. Copyright © 1983 by Gloria Steinem. Copyright © 1984 by East Toledo Productions, Inc. Reprinted by Permission of Henry Holt and Company, Inc.

From *Bronx Primitive* by Kate Simon. Copyright © 1982 by Kate Simon. Used by permission of Viking Penguin, a division of Penguin Books USA Inc.

Copyright © 1981 by Leslie Marmon Silko. Reprinted from *Storyteller* by Leslie Marmon Silko, published by Seaver Books, New York, New York.

Excerpts from *Remembering the Bone House* by Nancy Mairs. Copyright © 1989 by Nancy Mairs. Reprinted by permission of HarperCollins Publishers, Inc.

Reprinted from *Writing a Woman's Life* by Carolyn G. Heilbrun, by permission of W. W. Norton & Company, Inc. Copyright © 1988 by Carolyn G. Heilbrun.

Reprinted from *A World of Light, Portraits and Celebrations*, by May Sarton, by permission of W. W. Norton & Company, Inc. Copyright © 1976 by May Sarton.

Excerpts from *Knock Upon Silence*, by Carolyn Kizer, 1965. Reprinted by permission of Doubleday.

Excerpts from *Composing a Life*, by Mary Catherine Bateson, 1989. Reprinted by permission of Atlantic Monthly Press.

Excerpts from "Some Talk About Autobiography: An Interview with Eudora Welty," by Sally Wolff. *The Southern Review* (Winter 1990): 80–88. Reprinted by permission of Sally Wolff.

Excerpts from *Between Women*, by Carol Asher, Louise DeSalvo, and Sara Ruddick, eds. Reprinted by permission of Routledge, Chapman and Hall, Ltd. © 1984.

for Dorothy Braham
and in memory of Luther Braham

◆ Contents ◆

◆ Acknowledgments ◆

My fascinations with women's life writing derive from at least two sources: my love of decoding my own family's past and my experiences as a teacher of autobiographical texts.

Spotting my predilection for journals and letters, for collecting old photos, diaries, and leather-backed family histories early on, my friends and family have grown accustomed to my passion for tracing the thin, blue lifelines of the past. My two favorite family photos are circa 1932 and 1941: the first, a photograph of my mother wearing a gold locket, taken at the time she was engaged to be married; the second, a snapshot of my father dressed in army fatigues, taken with his father at Pittsburgh's bustling and dark-vaulted Penn Station. I have many other photographs of my parents, ones more recent or more professionally composed. But I prefer these two because of their power to trigger "memory." Through them I can reconstruct my version of the emotional content of their stories: the unadulterated joy of the first where the horizon stretched like one long promissory note; the nervous vulnerability of the second where the horizon stretched only as far as the 82nd Infantry might march. I am, it would seem, an illustration of my own thesis.

Teaching courses in women's life writing has deepened my access to and appreciation for autobiography's extraordinary power to reflect, redefine, and activate others' lives. While I owe much to feminist theory and scholarship, it is to the "ideal readers" of women's literary autobiography at Allegheny College, Smith College, and the University of New Hampshire—not infrequently "nontraditional students"—that I owe the impetus for this book.

Some friends and colleagues deserve to be singled out for special thanks. I'm particularly indebted to: Beth Reynders, Sonya Jones, Lloyd Michaels, Sally Knapp, Andrew Ford, Kristin Woolever, Chris Shipley, Jean Kennard, and Michael DePorte. Suzanne Bunkers shared with me her love of women's diaries and the conviction that the texts themselves deserved to be "read." Gail Hornstein, Director, and several colleagues at the Five College Women's Studies Research Center at Mount Holyoke College provided a lively forum for the rehearsal of some of these ideas. May Sarton and Patricia Hampl answered questions about their work in an exchange of lengthy letters, probably fatiguing for them, certainly exhilarating for me. And by the simple luck of submission, I acquired Gloria Bowles as an editor and friend.

I owe special gratitude to Sue Braham Mullen and Pamela Peterson, true collaborators in this endeavor; theirs is an extraordinary generosity of mind and heart.

Crucial Conversations

....

Interpreting Contemporary American Literary Autobiographies by Women

....

◆ Introduction ◆

Scholars working within both the humanities and the social sciences have persistently challenged the male, white, upper-class model of "achievement and quest" that dominated the field of biography and autobiography until the past 20 years. *Whose* lives, they ask, have been studied as exemplary, and what enlargements of our understanding of human experience can occur when "different" (women, blacks, working class, gay and lesbian) life experiences are included?

Women's personal narratives are essential primary documents, both as they expand the circumference of an autobiographical experience and as they provide the data for feminist research—particularly in the areas of personality development and values, historical and literary contributions. Some women's narratives reveal what their authors believe they are supposed to feel; their formulae acknowledge the conformist power of the dominant culture. Eudora Welty's *One Writer's Beginnings*, for example, documents exactly the sunny, uncomplicated, and uneventful childhood her fiction disputes. Sylvia Plath's *Letters Home* testify to the terrible power of the myth of the All American Girl: dutiful daughter, *summa* Smithie, perfect wife, fulfilled mother; a portrait not even her mother, to whom they were addressed and a powerful ally in the myth, could believe. Other women's narratives speak of ways the dominant culture marginalizes those not conforming to its conventions and assumptions. Audre Lorde, Adrienne Rich, and May Sarton offer life experience that counterpoints the dominant melodic line. Their very defiance of the "rules" reveals aspects of the system they wish to challenge or enlarge.

My investigation focuses on late-twentieth-century American literary artists, many of whom begin their careers as poets, who see the sharing of their life stories as a crucial part of their literary mandate. May Sarton, Adrienne Rich, Audre Lorde, Nancy Mairs, Patricia Hampl, Annie Dillard, Sylvia Plath, Anne Sexton, Maxine Kumin, Maya Angelou, Alice Walker, Kathleen Norris, Gloria Wade-Gayles, Leslie Silko: All receive initial critical acclaim as poets. Others in this study, who might not think of themselves as poets per se, habitually advance meaning via metaphor: Lillian Hellman's concept of "pentimento" or Toni Morrison's notion of memory's "flooding" are examples of the way meaning completes itself associatively rather than linearly. Metaphoric meaning—with its pluralistic possibilities reverberating in any given reader—is a means of moving many readers in a similar, if not absolutely identical, direction. Arguably then, the movement from poetry to memoir is a natural one: The power to speak to a wide readership may be effected through metaphor's powers to universalize and particularize simultaneously.

Since women's life writings exploded with particular intellectual and emotional energy in the 1970s and 1980s in America, my first chapter explores the points of intersection between these narratives and several highly influential texts in feminist discourse and theory. Widely read critical texts like Dinnerstein's *The Mermaid and the Minotaur*, Rich's *Of Woman Born*, and Miller's *Toward a New Psychology of Women* not only locate women's narratives on an exciting new playing field that redefines the roles of wife, mother, caregiver, scholar, artist, but also help to shape and sensitize a readership eager to play. One life experience has the potential to intersect with another and yet another, creating a network of "crucial conversations."[1]

The challenge of fracturing and discarding old ways of seeing oneself involves redefining the "truth content" of one's life experience. Chapters 2, 3, and 4 explore some of the complex layering inherent in truth-telling, particularly through the reflexive strategies of metaphor, memory, and a sense of place (geographic, emotional, cultural), which are used to construct a crafted reality. This created reality, temporarily accepted as "true on the page," is further qualified by the reader who also understands metaphor as "symbol" or "representation," memory as selective and relational, and a sense of place as a construct, one employing imagination as surely as fact. The reader then becomes a part of the discourse, resignifying the meaning of the text by returning, in Lacanian terms, "from the realm of the Imaginary to the Real." As my final chapter suggests, the reader becomes a collaborator in the truth content of the narrative by using the story as *exemplum* that enlivens and extends self-knowledge.

Jane Flax, in her provocative *Thinking Fragments: Psychoanalysis, Feminism, and Postmodernism in the Contemporary West* (1990), suggests that the use of multiple, intersecting frames of reference is probably the only adequate way of addressing questions of self, gender, knowledge, and power. Neither psychoanalytic theory, feminist theory, or poststructuralist theory is adequate on its own, she argues; new modes of thinking about the "self" and its values are effected only by stitching together "fragments" from each system and allowing them to converse with one another. Women's autobiography has always understood the need to compose a life from bits and pieces of the past marinated in memory, resurrected by the imagination and imbued with meaning. Studies in women's autobiography signal in their very titles this emphasis on process: *Composing a Life* (Mary Catherine Bateson), *Tapestries of Life* (Bettina Aptheker), *The Habit of Surviving* (Kesho Yvonne Scott), *Interpreting Women's Lives* (Personal Narratives Group, Eds.), *Writing a Woman's Life* (Carolyn Heilbrun), *Life/Lines* (Brodzki & Schenck, Eds.), *Writing Beyond the Ending* (Rachel DuPlessis).

Writing about women's autobiography in the past two decades has focused on the development of theoretical systems that can be employed as modes of inquiry into gender, power, class, and values. Clearly my own response to the autobiographies included in this study is informed by feminist theory and a critical stance toward classical psychoanalysis. Women's personal narratives have emphasized a revision of Oedipal dynamics and shifted emphasis from the paternal to the maternal. Collectively they relocate female desire and creativity, resignifying sources for the formation of identity and values. Uniformly they salute links among people, highlighting the *context* in which an action is performed, a goal achieved, a value defined, rather than portraying an isolated heroine surveying and reacting to her world. But, as Carolyn Heilbrun in a January 1990 lecture at Smith College remarked wryly, "We [cultural, historical, linguistic feminists] have many theories already and we risk ending up talking only to each other." Rather than adding to the already substantial body of theoretical discourse, I'd like to explore the implications of poetic patterns evident in these texts: strategies of self-inscription, explorations in memory, caught moments of "felt truth." And since poetic metaphor spirals into itself, readers can complete meaning associatively, becoming, in effect, extensions of the meaning of the text. This synchronicity between the author's transcribed life and the reader's empathic engagement gives autobiography its peculiar power.

Susan Stanford Friedman argues in her essay "Women's Autobiographical Selves" (1988) that the female self is never defined in isolation, although it often is examined in isolated crisis. The female autobiographical self, she contends, "does not oppose herself to all others, does not feel herself to exist outside of others, and still less against others, but very much *with* others in an interdependent existence that asserts its rhythm everywhere in the community." Friedman contrasts these terms of self definition with those found in standard male autobiography. Using Georges Gusdorf's widely read essay "Conditions and Limits of Autobiography" (1956) as a male exemplar, she writes:

> Women's autobiography comes as a literary tradition of self creation when we approach its texts from a psycho-political perspective based in the lives of women. Historically, women as a group have never been the "gatherers of men, of lands, of power, makers of Kingdoms or of empires" [Gus-

dorf's autobiographic requisites]. Instead, they have been the gathered, the colonized, the ruled. Seldom the "inventors of laws and wisdom," they have been born into those inventions. . . . All the more so if their race, religion, class, or sexual preference also marginalized them. Nonetheless, this historical oppression has not destroyed women's consciousness of self. (pp. 55–56)

And while I sometimes speak of shared traits, I do not wish to imply that women's personal narratives can be homogenized, distilled into a unitary, woman-identified iconography.[2] Beyond the commonalities of gender, historic time and place, and the capacity for artistic recollection, these are stories that celebrate diversity.

Diversity is also available in readers' responses, since the autobiographical act closes the circle of the "mirroring self" via the reader. Of course male *and* female authors incorporate a reader; reception theory has amply demonstrated in the past 20 years the variety and subtlety of these exchanges. And as John Clayton has argued in *Gestures of Healing: Anxiety and the Modern Novel* (1991), a surprising number of twentieth-century novelists—male and female—use the text as the "holding medium"— allowing, in the absence of a coherent sense of community, a fractured self to be completed. Writers, says Clayton, use the reader much as patients use an analyst; the collaboration between writer and reader functions in a therapeutic way, becomes a "gesture of healing."

Since women's identity is not only defined but, more significantly, *experienced* in connection, women's autobiography lays particular weight on the resonant reader as validator. The female autobiographical self is a "grounding of identity" through "linking with another consciousness." Jane Marcus in "The Private Selves of Public Women" (1988) identifies this consciousness as the reader's.

> If we agree that the writer resurrects herself through memory, then the reader also resurrects the writer through reading her. This *collaboration* is a reproduction of women's culture as conversation. It does not occur in the male model of individualistic autobiography, where the reader is not expected to take such an active role. (p. 137)

If the story of one woman's life provides a script the reader enters, resignifies, and in some collaborative sense makes her own, then contemporary women's personal narratives chart rich new possibilities for the ways women may want to live their lives. They present forms at once fragmentary and "contextual" enough to satisfy poststructuralist ideas about the "self" and powerful enough to link a reader's consciousness to the author's testimony. Their special strength lies in their implied or directly stated invitation to enter the text both imaginatively and analytically. The resulting self-authorization, the focus of the final chapter, empowers precisely because it activates another level of "received" response, the reader's, rather than putting closure on the author's past.

Finally, strict definitions of autobiography are stretched to include memoirs, "portraits," journals, letters, and essays, since they seem inter-penetrating and mutually enriching forms of self-inscription. Just as genre cannot be defined by aesthetic criteria alone, autobiographical truth is not defined solely by fidelity to factual data. Lillian Hellman's "adjustments" of history in her memoirs, for example, have been attacked as "untruthful," even as she suggests that her process of creating texture, plumbing feelings, and exploring memory is an effort to arrive at psychological, not factual, truth. As Luisa Passerini says: "All autobiographical memory is true. It is up to the interpreter to discover in which sense, where, for which purpose" (Personal Narratives Group, 1989, p. 261).

Although, as poet Carolyn Kizer puts it in "Pro Femina," women writers

> Are the custodians of the world's best kept secret:
> Merely the private lives of one-half of humanity

the secret is getting out. The extraordinary proliferation of literary auto-biographies produced by American women in the past 20 years parallels the dramatic "tide of poetry" that compelled Alicia Ostriker to write *Stealing the Language: The Emergence of Women's Poetry in America*. When women's literary autobiographies speak in such numbers and in such a constellation of arresting voices, they invigorate discussions about aesthetic criteria, genre boundaries, psychodynamic models, and their applications. They command attention just as, in their cumulative weight and insight, they carry their own emotional validations and spiritual incentives.

Margo Culley, in her Introduction to *American Women's Autobiography* (1992), summarizes the three major groupings into which those who currently engage in autobiographical critical discourse fall: critics of the "essentialist feminism" school, who argue that gender supersedes all other categories of definition, that the experience of being female yields a "global identity" (i.e., a common set of ways to know, to judge, to write); critics trained in language and the continental tradition, who emphasize the "plural subjectivities" of self, authorizing, and text; and critics who explore autobiographical traditions outside the dominant Anglo-American tradition (p. 4).

Implicit in all of these forums are the limits of what we can know of self, the limits of language, the instability of the text, the specific encoding of race, class, history, and culture. Yet I contend that even in the face of definers that fracture any notions of easy commonality, the autobiographical act mediates those limits by holding the pieces of a mosaic together with the glue of the recollected moment or within a striking metaphorical configuration.

Patricia Hampl observes that the autobiographical act springs from "the dry twigs left of a vanished life, whatever its fullness once was [which] are rubbed together until they catch fire. Until they make something. Until they make a story" (Sternburg, 1991, p. 30).

I'd like to explore some of those stories to see what makes them burn.

Notes

1 I use this term, originally the title of a novel by May Sarton, to refer to exchanges among texts and between author and reader in women's personal narratives.

2 In the past two decades, critics have provided abundant definitions of gendered characteristics useful in assessing women's autobiography: Nancy Chodorow (a female role orientation), Carol Gilligan (a female morality), Lillian Rubin, Nancy K. Miller, Jane Flax, Jane Gallop (a female approach in psychotherapy), Alicia Ostriker, Domna Stanton, Diane Wood Middlebrook, Marilyn Yalom, Adrienne Rich (a female sensibility), Patricia Meyer Spacks, Mary DeShazer, Catherine Portuges (a female imagination), Ellen Moers, Annette Kolodny, Sandra Gilbert, Susan Gubar, Gloria Bowles, Lillian Robinson, Elaine Showalter, Nina Baym (a female literary tradition), Estelle Jelinek, Lyn Lifshin, Suzanne Juhasz, Carolyn Heilbrun, Suzanne Bunkers, Margo Culley (a female autobiographical tradition), and Gloria Hull, bell hooks, Nellie McKay, Barbara Christian, Gloria Anzaldua (a female ethnic tradition). This discussion is indebted to their discoveries, many of which now appear as working assumptions in feminist research. I have not attempted to duplicate their methodology by contrasting women's descriptions of the past with male descriptions or the defined contours of male autobiography. It is women's narratives that have gone untold or unexamined too long, and it is that *oeuvre* I wish to treat.

◆ 1 ◆

Caregivers Redefined:
The Mother Bond

Women's life experience need not derive authorization via a single model or, in Domna Stanton's words, "a sacred text that seals our conversion for life." Rather, she argues in "Books That Changed Our Lives" (1991), "We do need sister texts with which we can have heated debates, even decades of disagreements—imperfect, provisional models that inscribe the strengths and blind spots of the past and thus of our own struggles as we see them" (p. 10).

The centrality of the mother–daughter relationship, embedded as it is in redefining the roles of caregivers, is one powerful source of the "heated debates" to emerge from a variety of "sister texts" in the 1970s and 1980s. As child psychologists shifted from developmental models based on drives or ego psychology to object-relations, that is, how the child relates to those "objects" (persons) at the center of the emotional life he or she experiences, authors and the audiences targeted by their writings re-examined the roles of primary caregiver and mother–child interactions.

Psychologists stressed that attachments, relationships, become crucial determinants of the developing self and its health. What the child experiences and how he or she processes that experience shifts attention to the pre-Oedipal modes of connection. Mothers, overwhelmingly the primary caregivers through the 1960s, offer crucial arenas for study. Developmentalists not only locate in the mother–daughter bond the images of the self that are formed; they explain memory as a function not just of physiological circuitry but of emotional nurturance, and separation not as simple individuation (in the Oedipal sense of autonomy) but rather as "mature dependency."[1]

At the same time that developmental psychologists were studying the effects of the mother bond, popular culture was romanticizing "good mother" roles and vilifying "bad mother" stereotypes. Attempts to describe mother–child interactions, and to trace their effects, when stripped of their

7

subtleties and complex interconnections, could be reduced in the media to simplistic "mother-blaming theories."

Moving Away From Good Mother/Bad Mother Stereotypes

In 1976 three powerful, wide-ranging critical studies were published, each examining the complexity of maternal experience and feeling, each challenging reductive theories of "mothering": Jean Baker Miller's *Toward a New Psychology of Women*, Dorothy Dinnerstein's *The Mermaid and the Minotaur*, and Adrienne Rich's *Of Woman Born*. Each volume emphasizes the primacy of the mother bond. Miller derives a new female developmental model based on self-in-relation theories; Dinnerstein demonstrates that until primary care responsibilities are shared more equally by both sexes, our "sexual malaise" will continue; Rich studies motherhood as an "institution," one the patriarchy manipulates to subjugate women. A scant two years later Nancy Chodorow's volume, *The Reproduction of Mothering*, appears, stressing the differences apparent in the ways sons and daughters are mothered; how, in effect, gender socialization operates.

Jean Baker Miller's *Toward a New Psychology of Women* initiated a re-examination of gender stereotypes, demonstrating that female traits previously devalued in Freudian theory were, instead, unique and socially valuable strengths. Women in our culture are the "carriers" of certain aspects of the human experience—for example, emotionality, vulnerability, nurturance, and empathy for others. The development of empathy is a trait experienced in the mother–daughter relationship. The mother "mirrors" the infant during its earliest stages of nurturance. Since mothers and daughters are more closely identified (anatomical sameness) than mothers and sons, a mother may feel more comfortable about encouraging a daughter to feel intimately connected to her, the rehearsal for emotional intimacy with others. Nancy Chodorow extends this point by demonstrating that women's relational capacities stem directly from differences in the way mothers "mirror" their sons and daughters. Boys are encouraged to separate decisively from their mothers. Girls are seen as extensions of their mothers and thereafter display more permeable ego boundaries as well as "ambivalent" attachments to their mothers in adult life. A female conception of "self" is defined by "connections" to others. Further, emotional difficulties can develop when young women's basic relational needs are not given recognition and "avenues for development are ignored or misinterpreted as dependent behaviors."[2]

Dorothy Dinnerstein, in *The Mermaid and the Minotaur*, underscores the primacy of the mother's care in dictating all our subsequent sexual arrangements. Arguing that within our current child-care system females "mono-polize" infant nurturance, "the central infant–parent relationship, in which we form our earliest, intense and wordless, feelings toward existence, is a relation with a woman." Rather than valorizing this exchange, or seeing it as a medium of emphatic rehearsal for the female infant, Dinnerstein indicts this system, characterizing it as terminally ill, suffering from and producing more "sexual malaise." Female-dominated child care unleashes an unhealthy chain of consequences on both male and female that include: male insistence upon and female compliance with a double standard of sexual behavior; male fear of "engulfment" and female fear of autonomy; a fear of female authority, and male-based cultural assumptions that view women "as an asset to be owned and harnessed, harvested and mined" (pp. 236–237).

Adrienne Rich in *Of Woman Born: Motherhood as Experience and Institution* looks not only at the individual mother–child bond, but more particularly at the institution of motherhood and its historic struggle with male authority. In exposing the manipulations of the institution of motherhood, her "real subject" becomes patriarchal power and its desire (sometimes conscious, sometimes unconscious) to subjugate women.

There is no such thing as value-free knowledge, Rich argues. From its base of political power, the dominant group in society assumes the responsibility and authority for disseminating knowledge and values. For example, when, during the Middle Ages, the church controlled virtually all aspects of society, any knowledge that threatened or disputed its view of the world was suppressed. Similarly, in the five thousand years of patriarchal culture, knowledge about the role, status, or function of women has been formulated and disseminated via patriarchal standards. Not surprisingly, Rich concludes that in order to sustain male privilege, mother-hood has been manipulated to limit female potential. Her data base includes not only historic surveys and statistics, but her own experience of being a daughter and a mother.

The cumulative message of these four studies is the testimony, through a variety of perspectives, about the centrality of nurturance as it colors female experience. Strategies for forming a "self" are based on connections rather than separations; they are rehearsed first in the mother–daughter relationship; they can be recovered only by a deconstruction of patriarchal history and a dismantling of "gender malaise."

Readers of these texts were alerted to the insidious power of silencing. Our dominant culture does have clear "good mother"/"bad mother" stereotypes, they argued, and, as Alicia Ostriker puts it in *Stealing the Language* (1986), female writers struggle against amnesia and denial. Good mother, in our culture, is selfless, cheerful, and deodorized. It does not include resentment, anger, violence, alienation, disappointment, grief, fear, exhaustion—or erotic pleasure. . . . Our culture does not give us images of a daughter desperate for a mother's love, or desperate to escape it, or contemptuous of the mother, nor do we have an archetype of the Prodigal Daughter who escapes and returns. (pp. 179–180)

Portraits of Mothers and Nurturers

It is precisely those images that female autobiographers began to supply in the 1970s. Vivian Gornick draws the portrait of a mother whose engulfing tentacles produce "fierce attachments"; Maxine Hong Kingston's mother releases her daughter's own subversive imagination; in Kim Chernin's "mother's house," Kim's story can be retrieved only by uncovering the story of the "favored daughter," the dead Nina. Fathers are sometimes included in the childhood drama—frequently the shadowy, marginalized figures of the Dinnerstein model but, at other times, the role model a writer like the young May Sarton patterns her values around, even as she mimics his rages, which she terms "infantile" and "destructive." In every instance, however, the goal the daughter seeks is not separation and autonomy as described by Freud, but autonomy *and* attachment, the Miller paradigm.

Since autobiography fingers many of childhood's most powerful memories, some of the most poignant data about mothers, mothering, and mother–daughter relationships emerge in female autobiography. "We think back through our mothers, if we are women," declares Virginia Woolf, and her remark could be suspended equally fruitfully over the psychological-emotive-cognitive process of memory, the mirroring of the self via the nurturing primary caregiver, or the constraints placed on the institution of motherhood by patriarchal culture. Interest in new and more complex definitions of mother–child interactions occurs almost simultaneously with a rapidly growing number of female autobiographies in which the portrait and influence of a mother figure are central.

If, as Paul John Eakin (1985) and James Olney (1972) have postulated in a persuasive series of essays on the autobiographical act, autobiography is less a "record of an already completed self" than a process, a "drama of self definition," that drama is frequently played out in the presence of the mother. Mothers are foregrounded in writers as diverse as Maxine Hong Kingston, Alice Walker, Maya Angelou, Vivian Gornick, Gloria Steinem, and Kim Chernin. Kingston, Walker, Angelou, and Steinem use the autobiographical act to "break silence," to articulate what normative social conventions have sought to repress, deny, or simply avoid. Mary McCarthy and Lillian Hellman, the first a literal orphan, the second a culturally displaced person, emphasize what the child substitutes for the mother and, more poignantly, the role memory plays in filling the parental gaps with "recalled" childhood experience. Vivian Gornick and Kim Chernin animate portraits of mothers so powerful that their stories threaten to eclipse the narratives of their daughters. Theirs is a power struggle.

Fathers are occasionally present in these childhood dramas, usually standing off- or upstage, figures to be reckoned with but rarely encountered. (One thinks of Tennessee Williams's technique in "The Glass Menagerie" of spotlighting the portrait of the absent father—a crucial presence in family dynamics, but one who early on "fell in love with long distance.") Fathers in these texts could be described in the terms Dinnerstein suggests: They are the logical consequences of our "gender malaise." Shadowy figures, displaying little affect, occasionally bullies but more frequently benign despots, they are reliable for financial support but rarely accessible emotionally. In May Sarton's portraits of her parents, however, the father is the figure who represents access to the wider world that May, as a writer, wishes to claim. Although her mother's life is subsumed by his obsessive 18-hour-a-day work patterns, *his rituals* are the ones Sarton will replicate in her life story.

The autobiographies of Angelou, Steinem, Chernin, Gornick, McCarthy, Hellman, and Sarton describe childhoods and parenting practices in the 1930s, 1940s, and 1950s—precisely the data base Dinnerstein, Rich, and Miller use in constructing their critiques. One might argue that the alterations of the 1970s, 1980s, and 1990s—particularly in *broadening* the definitions of "primary caregiver"—might relegate these portraits to the category of interesting historical footnotes.[3] But the difficulties peculiar to the formation of a female self, particularly how the female child establishes some sense of herself as an "entity" while still incorporating the needs of others and honoring the influence of parents and peers, are always acute. It is a precarious "balancing act," Jean Baker Miller suggests, regardless of the slow alterations in parenting practices. Also evident in the "balance" is the interactive nature of the exchange between child and parent. Daughters are not simply recipients of pressures from their mothers, any more than mothers passively conform to culturally sanctioned roles. These are narratives that accord the child energy and intentionality as well as equipping the mother with power.

Kim Chernin's *In My Mother's House* (1983) and Vivian Gornick's *Fierce Attachments* (1987) describe precarious "balancing acts" in worlds almost identical in specific locale and emotional atmosphere. The Jewish immigrant experience is their mothers' story: Both mothers are strong-willed

Russian Jews, liberal thinkers, distinguished by a fierce sense of self and personal integrity. Consequently, the towering figures of the mothers become the apparent real subject of each text. As one reads, however, one discovers that Chernin and Gornick, in telling their mothers' stories, are also separating themselves from its authority and dominance. Chernin offers *In My Mother's House* as a mother to daughter exchange; she begins the volume by asking her mother, Rose, to tell her story; discovers in Rose's story, her own; and passes along this volume to her daughter, Larissa. Similarly, Vivian Gornick offers the story of her mother—her obsessive need for love, her push-me-pull-me independence–dependence dynamic— as a "fierce attachment" in need of release; mother and daughter must relieve one another of its bondage.

> My relationship with my mother is not good, and as our lives accumulate it often seems to worsen. We are locked into a narrow channel of acquaintance, intense and binding. For years at a time there is an exhaustion, a kind of softening, between us. Then the rage comes up again, hot and clear, erotic in its power to compel attention. These days it is bad between us. My mother's way of "dealing" with the bad times is to accuse me loudly and publicly of the truth. Whenever she sees me she says, "You hate me. I know you hate me." I'll be visiting her and she'll say to anyone who happens to be in the room—a neighbor, a friend, my brother, one of my nieces—"She hates me. What she has against me I don't know, but she hates me." She is equally capable of stopping a stranger on the street when we're out walking and saying, "This is my daughter. She hates me." Then she'll turn to me and plead, "What did I do to you, you should hate me so?" I never answer. I know she's burning and I'm glad to let her burn. Why not? I'm burning, too.
>
> But we walk the streets of New York together endlessly. We both live in lower Manhattan now, our apartments a mile apart, and we visit best by walking. My mother is an urban peasant and I am my mother's daughter. The city is our natural element. We each have daily adventures with bus drivers, bag ladies, ticket takers, and street crazies. Walking brings out the best in us. I am forty-five now and my mother is seventy-seven. Her body is strong and healthy. She traverses the island easily with me. We don't love each other on these walks, often we are raging at each other, but we walk anyway. (pp. 6–7)

Gornick takes readers into that territory where mothers and daughters struggle, separate, reconcile, try to talk, sometimes love one another inordinately, and sometimes devour one another alive.

Their struggle revolves around several key issues, understood differently by each: the nature of love, the response to grief, the obligation to family. The issues, of course, are all interconnected, bound up in nurturance, and the responses to circumstances a harsh life deals out.

The harshest fact of her mother's life, as Gornick sees it, is the premature death of a much-loved husband. Good-looking, compassionate, a romantic in an unromantic world, Gornick's father dies unexpectedly of three heart seizures when he is 51. Her mother is 46, her brother 19, and she 13 at that time.

> When the doorbell rang my brother was the first one out of bed, Mama right behind him, and me behind her. We all pushed into the tiny foyer. My brother stood in the doorway beneath the light from a sixty-watt bulb staring at a pale-yellow square of paper. My mother dug her nails into his arm. "Papa's dead, isn't he? Isn't he?" My brother slumped to the floor, and the screaming began.
>
> "Oh," my mother screamed.
>
> "Oh, my God," my mother screamed.
>
> "Oh, my God, help me," my mother screamed.
>
> The tears fell and rose and filled the hallway and ran into the kitchen and down across the living room and pushed against the walls of the two bedrooms and washed us all away. . . . My only hope was retreat. I went unresponsive, and I stayed that way. (pp. 62–63)

Seeing herself as "a prop in the extraordinary drama of Mama's bereavement" (p. 64), Gornick suggests that much of her mother's ensuing behavior and the effects of that behavior on her children flows from her conviction that with her husband's death, "something had occurred we were not to support, not to live through, or at the very least be permanently stunted by" (p. 65).

Fierce Attachments describes how Gornick overcomes the feeling that "disaster seemed imminent rather than already accomplished" (p. 66). At first, her coping mechanisms are the simple requirements of getting through the day with a mother whose "grief was [so] primitive and all encompassing: it sucked the oxygen out of the air" (p. 54). Later, she is able to see how personal circumstance is reinforced by Jewishness, its history of abandonments and victimizations intensifying personal grief. It's all a chronicle of griefs. And still later she is able to find her mother's fears of abandonment replicated in her own, her mother's fantasy of rescue duplicated in her own failed love affairs and sad attempts at marriage with what her mother sees as one schlemiel after another. As education, analysis, and geographic separation enable her to come to terms with the blueprint her mother's life has made for her own, she is able to transcend some of its crueler boundaries.

> We always walked, she and I. We don't always walk now. We don't always argue, either. We don't always do any of the things we always did. There is

no always anymore. The fixed patterns are beginning to break up. This breakup has its own pleasures and surprises. (p. 193)

Although the habit of "accusation and retaliation" remains strong in their relationship, Gornick's book ends with a testament of acceptance. "We have survived our common life, if not together at least in each other's presence, and there is a peculiar comradeship between us now" (p. 200). The book creates "a degree of distance." And "this little bit of space provides me with the intermittent but useful excitement that comes of believing I begin and end with myself" (p. 200).

Kim Chernin's mother, Rose, is as dominating a presence as Vivian Gornick's "Mama." She humbles by her achievement and humanity rather than enslaving her daughter by her needs. *In My Mother's House* alternates sections of Rose's story (The First Story My Mother Tells: Childhood in Russia or America, the Early Years) with Kim's (The First Story I Tell: Hard Times, The Second Story I Tell: A Communist Childhood). Her motive in structuring the book in this way seems at least twofold: to preserve the life of Rose Chernin, a passionate leftist whose shetetl beginnings flower into a rich political life caught by these mementos in her apartment.

> A charcoal sketch of Harriet Tubman, given by Langston Hughes . . . and a plaque that reads: "To ROSE CHERNIN FOR 25 YEARS OF MILITANT LEADERSHIP TO THE COMMITTEE FOR THE DEFENSE OF THE BILL OF RIGHTS. IN APPRECIATION OF YOUR LIFELONG DEVOTION AND STRUGGLE ON BEHALF OF THE FOREIGN-BORN OF ALL VICTIMS OF POLITICAL AND RACIAL OPPRESSION." (pp. 11–12)

Kim Chernin's second purpose is to record her own life, one shared with this fascinating and equally terrifying figure (Rose Chernin is jailed repeatedly during her long history of protests—once for six months, when Kim is 11), to derive its meanings and to pass it along as a legacy to her daughter. The book begins and ends with the epithet "from mother to daughter" and it is dedicated

> For my mother, Rose Chernin
> For her mother, Perle Chernin
> And for my daughter, Larissa Chernin.

The *rite de passage*, then, is a continuing and ongoing process reinforced by the cyclical stories that form the core of the book.

> I learned to understand my mother's life when I was a small girl, waiting for her to come home in the afternoons. Each night I would set the table care-

fully, filling three small glasses with tomato juice while my father tossed a salad. Then we would hear my mother's car pull up in front of the house and I could go into the living room and kneel on the gray couch in front of the window to watch her come across the lawn, weighed down with newspapers and pamphlets and large blue boxes of envelopes for the mailing I would help to get out that night.

She was a woman who woke early, no matter how late she went to bed the night before. Every morning she would exercise, bending and lifting and touching and stretching, while I sat on the bed watching her with my legs curled up. Then, a cold shower and she would come from it shivering, smelling of rosewater, slapping her arms. She ate toast with cottage cheese, standing up, reading the morning paper. But she would always have too little time to finish her coffee. I would watch her taking quick sips as she stood at the door. "Put a napkin into your lunch," she'd call out to me, "I forgot the napkin." And there was always a cup with a lipstick stain standing half full of coffee on the table near the door.

Later, the Party gave her a car and finally she learned how to drive it. But in the early years she went to work by bus. Sometimes when I was on vacation I went downtown with her.

In her office she took off her shoes and sat down in a wooden chair that swiveled. Always, the telephone was ringing. A young black man. Framed on a false murder charge. And so she was on her feet again, her fist clenched. By twelve o'clock she would have made friends with the young man's mother. And for years after that time some member of his family would drive across town on his birthday to pick up my mother and take her home to celebrate.

. . . She was born in a village where most women did not know how to read. She did not see a gaslight until she was twelve years old. And I? Am I perhaps what she herself might have become if she had been born in my generation in America? (pp. 14–15)

Untorn by the competition Gornick feels with her mother, Chernin "tak[es] down her tales with all the skill available to me as a writer." This does not delimit Kim's story, but stitches it to a longer, archetypal story of "women of the world who survive all terrible circumstances." When the book progresses to the point that Kim is born, the mantle is simply passed to her. "You begin to grow up, you take your place in the family," her mother says. "You must start talking. What happens in my life after this, who I am, what sort of person I am in the world, we must hear later from you" (p. 184). The nexus between Rose's story and Kim's is not, in fact, Kim's birth; it is the birth and tragic death of the other child, Nina—poetic, talented—who, at 16, dies a painfully protracted death from Hodgkin's disease.

414 East 204th Street
March 1980

"Nina is dead." I say these words I have avoided for a lifetime, and which
were never spoken to me when I was a child. I repeat them, beneath my
breath, then louder. I am walking by myself in the Bronx. If anyone looks at
me I pretend that I am humming to myself, or singing. "Nina is dead," forcing the words against my own numbness. It is a cold day, people are walking fast, tucking their necks down into their collars. I wrap a scarf around
my face. The wind is so strong I find it difficult to move forward. I hear the
sound of the subway roaring past, shaking the ground all around me. I feel
this same upheaval inside myself. I remember my mother's face, when she
had lived through Nina's death again with me. It looked small and pinched;
her eyes were timid. Then, she was weeping. A few tears at first, then more
and more of them. But her face never changed. It didn't crumple, or wrinkle,
she didn't sob or close her eyes. Her shoulders shook and I put my arms round
her. It was the first time she wept because of Nina. The first time in thirty-
five years. It was the beginning of mourning in our family because of Nina's
death. And for me it was the beginning of memory. (p. 199)

And so Kim's story begins, in the acknowledgment and grief for her sister's
death. Kim's story records some of the costs of being Rose Chernin's daughter, the child of an avowed communist during the Red Scare, blacklisted,
jailed, vilified in newspapers. As she records these painful years, she and
her mother confront truths they have evaded earlier.

So that's it? That's why she withdrew? I should have known it. She
has carried this guilt, as a mother, even before I was born. This awful sense
that she has hurt her children by being a Communist. But I had wanted to
give her this story of our life as a gift; as a reparation even for Nina's death.
(p. 232)

In uncovering the "echo of lonely guilt and horror that always until now
divided us" (p. 233), Kim and her mother are freed to know one another.
Together they trace her McCarthy hearings experience, her threatened
deportation—assessing how it felt to mother and how it felt to child.
Kim Chernin threads her adolescence, her own self-styled rebellions, tri-
umphs, schooling at Berkeley, aspirations to be a writer, marriage, around
and through the fabric of her mother's life—each life commenting on the
other.

     Their conflicts are intense, like their love—the recurrent and key con-
frontation occurring over Kim's desire "not to be a political person but to
be a poet." Her mother's reply: "That's all we need, another poet, and the
world at the edge of a holocaust" (p. 283). Their confrontations, angry and

passionate, serve, ultimately, as avenues of approach rather than reproach, and the final pages of *In My Mother's House* are filled with the forgiveness that ensures a future.

The catharsis so apparent in the "Nina Story" also fuels Gloria Steinem's "Ruth's Song" (in *Outrageous Acts and Everyday Rebellions*, 1983), a portrait of a mother who is tortured and torturing because of recurrent bouts of mental illness. Not only does Steinem wish to release herself from the pain and childhood humiliation of her mother's disease and isolation—to provide a "medium" of forgiveness as Gornick and Chernin do—she also wishes to address readers who have parallel experiences. More self-consciously than either Gornick or Chernin, Steinem invites the reader into her text, drawing parallels when appropriate.

Notice how the opening paragraph of "Ruth's Song" invites the reader into self-assessment.

> Happy or unhappy, families are all mysterious. We have only to imagine how differently we would be described—and will be, after our deaths—by each of the family members who believe they know us. The only question is, why are some mysteries more important than others? (p. 129)

Steinem goes on to answer her own question (as readers ponder their own) by suggesting that the fate of her Uncle Ed was the "mystery of importance in our family" (p. 129). A brilliant electrical engineer full of promise, he was transformed by the end of his life into a broken, oft-sneered-at town handyman, and speculations about his "fall" ranged from Depression "casualty," to mental problems, to intellectual experimentations with socialism. Uncle Ed was the subject of interest, discussion, and explanatory theory all his life; as Adrienne Rich suggests in *Of Woman Born*, patriarchal privilege assumes that male authority, when compromised, is the source of serious interest and inquiry.

No such scrutiny attended Steinem's mother, even when she, too, suffered a radical transformation from a fun-loving, scholarship-winning, adventuresome Oberlin freshman to a "terrorized woman who tried hard to clean our littered house whenever she emerged from her private world, but who could rarely be counted on to finish one task" (p. 130).

In examining her mother's slide from independent woman into terrorized invalid, Steinem does not disguise either the anger or shame of being her child. Neither does she dismiss Ruth with the blanket diagnosis: mentally ill. Instead, Ruth becomes the "important mystery" worth examining in her family, and in "singing Ruth's song" Steinem uncovers powerful social and cultural constraints that help her understand, forgive, and come to terms with Ruth's dilemma.

Unlike the case of my uncle Ed, exterior events were never suggested as reason enough for her problems. Giving up her own career was never cited as her personal parallel of the Depression. (Nor was there discussion of the Depression itself, though my mother, like millions of others, had made potato soup and cut up blankets to make my sister's winter clothes.) Her fears of dependence and poverty were no match for my uncle's possible political beliefs. The real influence of newspaper editors who had praised her reporting was not taken as seriously as the possible influence of one radical professor. Even the explanation of mental illness seemed to contain more personal fault when applied to my mother. (p. 131)

Surely a part of Ruth's silence is attributable, as Steinem reconstructs it, to the fact that she is a woman, one not expected to excel in a career—but, if she insists on having one, expected to juggle it successfully with being a good wife and mother. Her failures in the last two roles stigmatize her and block efforts to relieve or penetrate her world of increasing confusion and terror.

While Steinem is compassionate about Ruth's plight, she is as vividly honest in confronting the humiliation of being her child. Perhaps most onerous is the constant responsibility it creates, depriving her of a childhood and requiring that she care for, in fact, "mother her mother." The pain and sadness of her mother's life, ill-defined because Steinem as yet does not have the distance that confers perspective on it, are replaced by the small and large humiliations of being her child. At times her mother, waking up in a dark house, forgets the after-school job her daughter always maintains and, in her disorientation and fear, calls in the police to search for her. At other times the medicine she takes to control depression slurs her speech and impedes her gait to the point that Steinem's teenage friends think her mother is drunk. Mostly, her oppressive *thereness* is what confines the young Steinem who, alone with her mother between the ages of 10 and 17, has always her quaking, agoraphobic world to return to or to feel guilty about escaping from for a few hours each day.

"Pity takes distance and a certainty of surviving" (p. 135), Steinem observes, and she acquires distance only when she goes to live with her older sister in Washington and Ruth is placed in a mental hospital in Baltimore, "a humane place with gardens and trees where I visited her each weekend of the summer" (p. 136). Under the care of good doctors for the first time in her life, a new Ruth emerges, one who begins to talk about her past life, her childhood, her scholarship to Oberlin, her marriage to a funny, charming if "unacceptably Jewish" young man, her career in journalism. She traces the strain of a job, a marriage, and two young babies to its final eruption in a breakdown. Although Steinem concedes that other women, even women of her mother's generation, could have resolved these conflicts more successfully than her mother, she recounts a story her mother told again and again that "symbolized for me the formidable forces arrayed against her" (p. 138).

> It was early spring, nothing was open yet. There was nobody for miles around. We had stayed at the lake that winter, so I was alone a lot while your father took the car and traveled around on business. You were a baby. Your sister was in school, and there was no phone. The last straw was that the radio broke. Suddenly it seemed like forever since I'd been able to talk with anyone—or even hear the sound of another voice.
>
> I bundled you up, took the dog, and walked out to the Brooklyn road. I thought I'd walk the four or five miles to the grocery store, talk to some people, and find somebody to drive me back. I was walking along with Fritzie running up ahead in the empty road—when suddenly a car came out of nowhere and down the hill. It hit Fritzie head on and threw him over to the side of the road. I yelled and screamed at the driver, but he never slowed down. He never looked at us. He never even turned his head.
>
> Poor Fritzie was all broken and bleeding, but he was still alive. I carried him and sat down in the middle of the road, with his head cradled in my arms. I was going to *make* the next car stop and help.
>
> But no car ever came. I sat there for hours, I don't know how long, with you in my lap and holding Fritzie, who was whimpering and looking up at me for help. It was dark by the time he finally died. I pulled him over to the side of the road and walked back home with you and washed the blood out of my clothes.
>
> I don't know what it was about that one day—it was like a breaking point. When your father came home, I said: "From now on, I'm going with you. I won't bother you. I'll just sit in the car. But I can't bear to be alone again." (p. 139)

This tale seems almost Kafkaesque, the tragic case of life imitating art. Fritzie, the surrogate child who can't be protected, the absent father/husband, the abandoned mother/wife, the impotence and terror that paralyze, the crushing dependency that results—all seem like "proofs" in a Dinnerstein model pushed to nightmare.

Although Steinem would *like* to "tell you this story has a happy ending," her mother's fears were to return, requiring one more extended hospitalization, and agoraphobia all her life. Yet her old age was less terrifying than her young adulthood and middle age, and she continued to show flashes of a wry sense of humor, a love of learning, and a respect for writing. Steinem knows she "will spend the next years figuring out what her life has left in me." Already she notices an empathy with old people and with children of "crazy parents," not to mention a lifelong commitment to equal rights for women, equal attention to their issues, needs, and care. Steinem turns her last lines outward to the reader.

> I miss her, but perhaps no more in death than I did in life. Dying seems less sad than having lived too little. But at least we're now asking questions about all the Ruths and all our family mysteries. If her song inspires that, I think she would be the first to say: It was worth the singing.

In Ruth's "mystery" and poignancy lies the metaphor we can stretch to fit our own families, their missed opportunities. Perspective is what allows the attachment.

Perspective is what Alice Walker examines in her essay "Beauty: When the Other Dancer Is the Self" (*In Search of Our Mothers' Gardens*, 1983). The youngest child of five boys and three girls born to Georgia sharecroppers Willie Lee and Minnie Lou Walker, she recounts a period in her childhood when she is the prettiest, the "babychild" to be honored with rare trips in a car or chosen to recite Easter speeches in church. "It was great fun being cute. But then, one day, it ended" (p. 386).

At 8 years old she is playing cowboys and Indians with her brothers. Relegated to the role of an Indian because she is a girl, she is accidentally hit in the eye by a pellet from a brother's BB gun. Admonished to remain silent, she lies to protect her brothers, claiming to have been hit by a branch. A week later when her pain level requires a trip to the doctor, she is told she will always be blind in that eye. The eye, which is disfigured with scar tissue and "wandering," causes her to retreat, a premature outcast. Even later when her most compassionate brother, Bill, arranges for surgery to remove the scar tissue, she continues to feel its shame and ugliness even though there is only a "tiny blue crater" where the scar tissue was. Her withdrawal has its positive effects, however, since she becomes an avid reader, an observer of people and their interactions, and an attentive recorder of the extraordinary embedded within ordinary life.

Walker completes her essay "Beauty" with three vignettes that demonstrate how an accident that could have been disabling actually enables her to grow as a person and as a writer. One is her decision to be photographed for the cover of her latest book despite the fact that the eye "may wander." Her lover tells her not to worry about the appearance she presents to the world: "It will be straight enough" (p. 390). The second is her poem of thanks after having seen for the first time the beauty of the desert. "I might have missed seeing the desert: The shock of that possibility—and gratitude for over twenty-five years of sight—sends me literally to my knees" (p. 391).

The final perspective is provided by her 3-year-old daughter for whom Walker has waited, with some trepidation, to react to the eye and its scar.

> What will she say? Every day she watches a television program called "Big Blue Marble." It begins with a picture of the earth as it appears from the moon. It is bluish, a little battered-looking, but full of light, with whitish clouds swirling around it . . . one day when I am putting Rebecca down for her nap, she suddenly focuses on my eye. Something inside me cringes, gets ready to protect myself.
> . . . But no-o-o-o. She studies my face intently as we stand, her inside the crib and me outside. She even holds my face maternally between her dimpled little hands. Then, looking every bit as serious and lawyer-like as her father, she says, as if it may just possibly have slipped my attention, "Mommy, there's a world in your eye."
> . . . For the most part, the pain left then. (p. 393)

Coming to love and accept what is ours, turning potential disfigurement into an asset, and most particularly crediting her child with the capacity to identify what is "beauty" in a life are her survivor's strategies.

A recurring image of beauty in Walker's work is that of the individual who loves flowers and cultivates them even in the poorest soil. The growing of flowers under adverse conditions becomes symbolic of the mysterious transformations possible in human beings. The image, which she explores particularly in the essay "In Search of Our Mothers' Gardens," becomes her emblem for growing and living in spiritual beauty. Walker reasons that the stories she now tells are in fact her mother's stories, they are examples of what her mother and others like her might have created if they were not what Zora Neale Hurston (1935/1978) calls the "mules of the world" (p. 237) and had the opportunity to write, paint, or carve their own expressions. Although these women did not have access to art forms, they did create in whatever forms were allowed them. Walker sees this legacy of creativity as one of the spiritual bases of her own art.

> I notice that it is only when my mother is working in her flowers that she is radiant, almost to the point of being invisible—except as Creator: hand and eye. She is involved in work her soul must have. Ordering the universe in the image of her personal concept of Beauty.
> Her face, as she prepares the Art that is her gift, is a legacy of respect she leaves to me, for all that illuminates and cherishes life. She has handed down respect for the possibilities—and the will to grasp them. (p. 241)

Walker's mother created art as part of her daily life, as a force against the oppressive pressures of working in the fields, or as a maid, or as a full-time laborer who also raised eight children. Her metaphor is both intensely personal and intensely transpersonal. In the first instance, it is she who confers to the would-be poet and fictionist, her daughter, a sense of beauty and how to access it.

> Whatever she planted grew as if by magic, and her fame as a grower of flowers spread over three counties. Because of her creativity with flowers, even my memories of poverty are seen through a screen of blooms—sunflowers, petunias, roses, dahlias, forsythia, spirea, delphineums, verbena . . . and on and on. (p. 241)

But in a larger sense she also comes to represent an essential legacy in the lives of black women who, although denied formal access to the materials of art, used quilting, gardening, cooking, sewing to order their universe "in the image of their personal concept of beauty." What is passed along also helps define what survives, so "in searching for our mothers' gardens," Walker suggests we "also find our own."

Steinem's and Walker's essays pivot on portraits of mothers whose stamina and internal strength prevail (although sometimes cracking in the effort) over incredible odds. In studying their mothers these authors not only gain access to important formative influences in their own lives, but also widen the applicability of the story to include the reader.

If Steinem's and Walker's mothers provide a kind of "truth value" around which and against which childhood autobiographical memory revolves, Maya Angelou in *I Know Why the Caged Bird Sings* (1969) and Maxine Hong Kingston in *The Woman Warrior* (1976) arrive at a personal sense of self by flexing an outsider consciousness. Who they are is determined by who they are not.

Angelou and Kingston are nurtured in an oral tradition, one dominated by mother figures. Angelou models herself as an autobiographer around the figure of Momma, her mother's mother, a woman who presides over the country general store in the black section of Stamps, Arkansas as its collector of griefs, releaser of tensions, dispenser of measures of flour and human dignity. Kingston models herself on her Chinese mother, a teller of "talk stories." Unlike her mother's traditional interpretations of stories about making the cultural journey from China to California, however, Kingston poses alternative readings—ones that see conduct, especially of women, that is *not* in strict conformity to Chinese traditions as "courageous rebellions."

The quest toward selfhood, so familiar in the literature of the West, is more hard-won in the Chinese-American context, just as Angelou's efforts at self-esteem must be wrung again and again from the wet cloth of low expectation offered by white society. Angelou and Kingston are fascinated by the possibilities of rebirth; each story, in fact, ends with a birth—a new identity that is both the product of the story and the process embedded within its telling.

Kingston opens *The Woman Warrior* with two "framing stories." The first, the story of "No Name Woman," is the forbidden story, the one "you must not tell . . . 'In China your father had a sister who killed herself. She jumped into the family well. We say that your father has all brothers because it is as if she had never been born'" (p. 3).

The shame of the aunt's situation is that, despite the fact that her husband of one night to whom she was married by proxy is long gone to America, she is clearly pregnant. Kingston tries to imagine the circumstances that must have occurred. Because she is a woman, her aunt must have had to oblige a man—probably not a stranger in her small village— who wanted sex with her. Her mother interrupts this train of thought with more information. When the aunt is about to give birth the village people (perhaps including the seducer—or even prompted by him) attack the family home and to avenge this woman's "crime," slaughter all the livestock, smash the house, scatter supplies, and mark the entire area with blood. "'Your aunt gave birth in the pigsty that night,'" Kingston's mother continues. "'The next morning when I went for water, I found her and the baby plugging up the family well'" (p. 5).

Kingston believes that her mother tells this story to her as a warning. "She tested our strength to establish realities" (p. 5).

If the first framing story conveys the power of victimization, the second framing story is about empowerment. The legend of a woman warrior named Fa Mu Lan, the woman who took her father's place in battle, is Kingston's way of imagining herself in powerful and commanding ways. After her mother relates the story

> . . . I followed my mother about the house, the two of us singing about how Fa Mu Lan fought gloriously and returned alive from war to settle in the village. I had forgotten this chant that once was mine, given me by my mother, who may not have known its power to remind. She said I would grow up a wife and a slave, but she taught me the song of the woman warrior, Fa Mu Lan. I would have to grow up a woman warrior. (p. 24)

With the story of the victim and the story of the woman warrior firmly in place, Kingston tells the story of her mother, Brave Orchid. She is the "Shaman," the healer, one who studied medicine in China but was forced to work with her husband in a steam laundry in America. She has special visions and resources. She also carries all of the restrictions of a traditionalist—binding her daughter's mind into the constraints of an older generation. In short, the mother is both survivor and innovator, the victim of a culture's prohibitions and the woman warrior.

Kingston's fourth story concerns Moon Orchid, her mother's sister, the "Second Aunt," who is brought from China to claim her husband. He left for America 20 years earlier, married, and established another life with an American wife and family. When Brave Orchid insists on tracking him down in Los Angeles, Moon Orchid is crushed with humiliation at his new life and slowly deteriorates into madness. "'The difference between mad people and sane people,' Brave Orchid explains to her children, 'is that sane people have variety when they talk-story. Mad people have only one story that they talk over and over'" (p. 184). Although Brave Orchid tries to calm her sister's fears and exorcise her demons, she finally has to commit her to a sanatorium where, ironically, she feels safe and dies quietly.

Kingston locates her own story in the intersection between her mother's story, an example of survival through change, and Second Aunt's story, an example of madness through stasis. In the imaginative story of the warrior woman, Kingston recognizes the mechanisms of survival as women; one of them, reinforced by her mother's example, hinges on the capacity to invent possibilities for change, to imagine oneself into other options.

The fifth section of the book, "A Song for a Barbarian Reed Pipe" is her own story woven in response to and differentiation from the others. Unlike "No Name Woman," Kingston will be named; she will speak her experience and have it count. Like "The Woman Warrior," she acknowledges that the inner life of the imagination is real. It empowers. It creates the necessary preconditions for change. Like her mother she will alter the conditions of her life for survival's sake lest she be caught and held in the talons of a predatory culture, dying alone like Second Aunt.

Kingston's own sense of self revolves around her efforts to speak. First they are physical: "My mother cut my tongue. She pushed my tongue up and sliced the frenum. Or maybe she snipped it with a pair of nail scissors" (p. 164). Her mother claimed that she performed the act so that "you will not be tongue-tied. Your tongue will be able to move in any direction" (p. 164). Kingston suspects, however, that her mother's real reason was closer to the Chinese proverb: "A ready tongue is an evil."

Whether emotionally censored or physically impaired, the young Kingston has "a terrible time talking." She is overtaken with silence or a cracking "pressed duck voice" that freezes her "even when I want to say 'hello' casually, or ask an easy question in front of the check-out counter, or ask directions of a bus driver" (p. 165).

She displaces her troubles with speech onto another elementary school child, a terrifyingly shy Chinese girl who is enabled by her family in her muteness. Outraged by this painful reminder of herself, Kingston traps the girl for hours in a school lavatory trying to force her to speak. Overcome with shame at her torture, Kingston finally must release the girl and face her own self-directed anger.

Chinese and American culture vie with terrible pushes and pulls in her childhood. She resists what she can, accommodates to what she must, until one day she discovers her mother and father are plotting to marry her off to one of the FOBS—"Fresh-Off-the-Boats," immigrants from China looking for wives. This insult finally and emblematically loosens her tongue and she confronts her mother with a list of grievances that she's been silently compiling over the years. "Be careful what you say. It comes true. I had to leave home in order to see the world logically, logic the new way of seeing. I learned to think that mysteries are for explanation" (p. 204).

Kingston's story does end, however, with "logical explanation." It ends with a final framing story, an imaginative metaphor for her own life. The story revolves around Ts'ai Yen, a poetess of old who at the age of 20 was captured in a barbarian raid. During her 12-year stay with the barbarians she had two children, but they were never permitted to speak Chinese or learn of her culture. As terrifying as the barbarians were, they had the capacity to make strange, high, yearning music on their flutes—a sound at night like "an icicle in the desert" (p. 208). At first Ts'ai Yen tries to escape from this haunting sound but one night

> the barbarians heard a woman's voice singing, as if to her babies, a song so high and clear, it matched the flutes. Ts'ai Yen sang about China and her family there. Her words seemed to be Chinese, but the barbarians understood their sadness and anger. (p. 209)

Just as Ts'ai Yen's songs transcend her circumstances, so when she is ransomed and transcribes her songs for "the Barbarian Reed Pipe" for the Chinese, Kingston reports, "it translated well."

It is with art's power to imagine another condition, to "translate well," that Kingston ends her volume. The "pressed duck voice" has converted to the long, high note hanging like an icicle on the desert.

Maya Angelou's personal story also serves as a mirror for her race and culture. *I Know Why the Caged Bird Sings* tells the story of Marguerite ("Ritie") Johnson, born in St. Louis in 1928 to Bailey and Vivian Baxter Johnson. When she was 3 and her brother Bailey was 4, they were sent by their divorced parents to live in Stamps, Arkansas, which Angelou describes this way: "[the same as] Chitlin' Switch, Georgia; Hang 'Em High, Alabama; Don't Let the Sun Set on You Here, Nigger, Mississippi." "High spots in Stamps were usually negative," she suggests, "droughts, floods, lynchings and death" (p. 40).

Angelou lives in Stamps for the next ten years, reared by her indomitable maternal grandmother, Annie ("Momma") Henderson. Annie keeps a country store, a rallying point and social gathering spot for black field workers, and lives by the motto, "work, duty and religion." Although a degree of subservience to whites is necessary for her survival, the young Ritie observes how her grandmother retains her own integrity and dignity. Annie, for example, secures help from a white dentist when Ritie develops a badly abscessed tooth. Although he'd "rather stick my hand in a dog's mouth than in a nigger's," Annie forces compliance by reminding him of an earlier favor. Her determination withers the opposition. Momma also refuses "relief" even during the Depression years, and demonstrates how to succeed at a small business by being both honest and shrewd.

When Ritie is 8 she's invited back to St. Louis for a brief stay with her mother, "beautiful, light-skinned with straight hair" Vivian. During that visit she is raped by her mother's boyfriend and retreats into the brooding, insular silence Kingston also spoke of in her childhood.

> I discovered that to achieve perfect personal silence all I had to do was to attach myself leechlike to sound. I began to listen to everything. I probably hoped that after I had heard all the sounds, really heard them and packed them down, deep in my ears, the room would be quiet around me. I walked into rooms where people were laughing, their voices hitting the walls like stones, and I simply stood still—in the midst of the riot of sound. After a moment or two, silence would rush into the room from its hiding place because I had eaten up all the sounds. (p. 73)

After briefly accepting her behavior as "post-rape, post-hospital affliction," doctors and nurses, then relatives, become exasperated by her refusal/inability to speak and ship her back to Momma.

Her silence, compounded by the fear and self-loathing the rape produced, continues for almost a year until "a lady threw me my first life line" (p. 77).

> Mrs. Bertha Flowers was the aristocrat of Black Stamps. She had the grace of control to appear warm in the coldest weather, and on the Arkansas summer days it seemed she had a private breeze which swirled around, cooling her. She was thin without the taut look of wiry people, and her printed voile dresses and flowered hats were as right for her as denim overalls for a farmer. She was our side's answer to the richest white woman in town. (p. 78)

More important than her physical appearance and impeccable man-ners to the young Ritie (who felt "like an old biscuit, dirty and inedible") was Mrs. Flowers's generosity of spirit. Gradually, by subtle attention, bits of advice, small compliments, Mrs. Flowers restores Ritie's self-esteem and with it, her voice. She serves Ritie tea and elegant cakes, talks about the authors Ritie is reading in school, reads aloud with her *A Tale of Two Cities*, and asks—shrewdly—for Ritie to memorize one of her favorite poems each week they meet. Her interest and encouragement pull the child back into a sense of self-worth, and her example suggests something worth reach-ing for.

In 1940, after Ritie's graduation at the top of her eighth-grade class, her fun-loving mother, now a professional gambler, moves the children from Stamps to San Francisco. The orderly, if "caged" world of Stamps is suddenly broken open.

> The air of collective displacement, the impermanence of life in wartime and the gauche personalities of the more recent arrivals tended to dissipate my own sense of not belonging. In San Francisco for the first time, I per-ceived myself as part of something. Not that I identified with the newcom-ers, nor with the rare black descendants of native San Franciscans, nor with the whites or even Asians, but rather with the times and the city. I under-stood the arrogance of the young sailors who marched the streets in ma-rauding gangs, approaching every girl as if she were at best a prostitute and at worst an Axis agent bent on making the USA lose the war. The under-tone of fear that San Francisco would be bombed which was abetted by weekly air raid warnings, and civil defense drills in school, heightened my sense of belonging. Hadn't I, always, but ever and ever, thought that life was just one great risk for the living?
>
> Then the city acted in wartime like an intelligent woman under siege. She gave what she couldn't with safety withhold, and secured those things which lay in her reach. The city became for me the ideal of what I wanted to be as a grownup. Friendly but never gushing, cool but not frigid or distant, distinguished without the awful stiffness. (p. 180)

This volume (there are several sequels) stops short of assessing whether or not Ritie achieves her "ideal." Her adventures in California include coming to terms with a colorful but alcoholic father, breaking the color line in applying for a streetcar conductorette, another try at school-ing, an illegitimate child. The child's birth, the last recorded episode of *Caged Bird*, ends the volume on a promissory note: "He was beautiful and mine. Totally mine" (p. 245). Afraid to disturb this "new perfection" in her life, Ritie protests when her mother insists the baby must sleep with her "to bond." Sure she will crush him in a moment of sleepy awkwardness, she tries at first to stay awake all night, but is overcome by sleep. Her mother wakens her gently some hours later asking her to look at her position and the baby's.

> Under the tent of blanket, which was poled by my elbow and forearm, the baby slept touching my side. Mother whispered, "See, you don't have to think about doing the right thing. If you're *for* the right thing, then you do it without thinking." (p. 246)

In the absence of formidable parental figures, Mary McCarthy and Lillian Hellman describe surrogate parents in *Memories of a Catholic Girlhood* (1957) and *An Unfinished Woman* (1969). As "orphans"—in McCarthy's case a literal orphan, in Hellman's a culturally displaced person—both authors are acutely aware of the unreliability of the accounts they construct and of how difficult it is to uncover or retrieve emotional truth. Because of this sensitivity, they employ techniques that interrupt the narrative flow, alerting the reader to the sifting, assessing function of memory. Hellman uses anecdotal flashbacks and "flashforwards" to suggest the play of memory on the materials of history. McCarthy employs passages that function as "voice-overs," often summarizing or highlighting sections of her narrative. The reader, then, is reminded periodically that she is entering *recollected* personal history, a writer's reconstruction of the formative influences on her life.

Lillian Hellman completed *An Unfinished Woman* in 1969 and it was warmly received as a modest and unassuming sketch of her life experiences. Some of the critical reaction that surrounded the volume pivots on what she chose to leave out: Her successes in the theatre, for example, are left virtually untouched. Hardly anyone challenges what she put in, though. Hellman herself repeatedly raised the subject of autobiographical "selection"—a subject she was to return to in *Pentimento* (1973) and *Scoundrel Time* (1976), sequels to this volume. When a later edition of her three memoirs appeared she wrote this in the Preface, characterizing the elusiveness of truth: "What a word is truth. Slippery, tricky, unreliable. I tried in these books to tell the truth, I did not fool with facts." *An Unfinished Woman* is peppered with references to Hellman's "trying to get it right," a process that suggests psychological veracity rather than historical accuracy. Because she is quick to admit uncertainty about certain facts and is possessed of less than total recall of some circumstances, the narrative gives the *feel* of candor and refreshing humility. It is precisely this "feel of honesty" that erupts in the "truth litigation" of *Pentimento* and *Scoundrel Time* and that plagues Lillian Hellman's final days—a subject I return to in a later chapter. [Hellman was engaged, at the time of her death, in a million dollar lawsuit against Mary McCarthy, who disputed the authenticity of the "facts" in *Pentimento* and *Scoundrel Time*.]

If we are to give Hellman her *donne*, that her purpose is to record recollected truth in the form of vignettes or portraits of some of the people who "formed her," then her "succinctness" and some of her "digressions" can better be understood. Occasionally she will summarize years of personal history in an epigrammatic line: "Mailer wasted time being famous," or, in referring to her love for Hammett, "[it was] the short cord that the years make into a rope." At other times she'll interrupt what appears to be a gripping moment in history with a quirky digression. For example, she stops her account of the 1937 visit to the Spanish War with a long anecdote about a crazy old man and his woman keeper whom she meets in a public park. Her encounters with the couple extend metaphorically the sense of the crazy, out of control, unpredictable political history in Europe in 1937, but she expects the reader to draw these parallels.

Lillian Hellman published *An Unfinished Woman* when she was 64. Her story begins conventionally with an account of her childhood in New Orleans in a middle-class Jewish family, a competitive collection of strong-willed relatives who collided in their attempts to shape the withdrawn, sensitive child. She countered with a retreat, a secret nest in a huge fig tree where she "could read and brood in private." Shuttled between New Orleans and New York every six months because of her father's work schedule, Hellman's was a life of constant adjustment: a dreamer in a family of materialists, a Jew in the South, a southerner in New York.

Like Angelou and Walker, her greatest affection was for nurturers—in her case her mother, whom she portrays as rather simple and open-hearted, somewhat bewildered by her husband's wheeler-dealer life, and more particularly two black women, Sophronia, her childhood nurse, and Helen, her housekeeper, both of whom are lovingly and luminously described.

Like McCarthy, Hellman discovers the gift for biting insight and gravitates toward mentors who cut through the "sophistications" and pretensions of the theatre and film communities of the 1930s. Most notable is her "cool teacher" Dashiel Hammett who put down almost everybody, taught her "how to write," embraced Marxism, and was her constant companion for almost 30 years. Another is Dorothy Parker, "a tangled fishnet of contradictions" whose celebrated wit and less well-documented sadness Hellman gets on the page. It is clear that Hellman has internalized the stubbornness and feisty integrity of both, yet she is also capable of recording their excesses, and the sad truth that the bottle got them.

Indeed it appears that the "consciousness of being alone" is what prompts Hellman, at 64, to open almost a decade of autobiographical assessment.

Hammett, the most vibrant presence in the volume, died in 1961, eight years earlier, after a period of deteriorating health, leaving her his literary executor. Dorothy Parker died on June 7, 1967, naming Hellman her executrix, a duty complicated by Parker's written request that literary proceeds from her estate pass directly to the NAACP. During the year immediately preceding publication of *An Unfinished Woman*, Hellman was trying to market *The Big Knockover*, a collection of Hammett's stories she had edited, and adjudicating Parker's difficult will. A "sense of being alone" could surely characterize such a time, just as the obligation to discharge duties to dead loved ones could prompt the vibrant portraits of Hammett and Parker in *An Unfinished Woman*. Miller's "autonomy and attachment" pattern is visibly played out in this script.

Mary McCarthy's *Memories of a Catholic Girlhood* (1957) takes on the elusive nature of autobiographical truth by directly addressing a long lead section "To the Reader" and subsequently interjecting direct address passages, "voice-overs" as it were, between sections of the narrative; she too ties the difficulty of substantiating "facts" to her orphanhood.

McCarthy says this about remembering "the substance of an event but not the details":

> Then there are cases where I am not sure myself whether I am making something up. I *think* I remember but I am not positive. I wonder, for instance, whether the Mesdames of the Sacred Heart convent really talked as much about Voltaire as I have represented them as doing; all I am sure of is that I first heard of Voltaire from the nuns in the convent. And did they really speak to us of Baudelaire? It seems to me now extremely doubtful, and yet I wrote that they did. I think I must have thrown Baudelaire in for good measure, to give the reader an idea of the *kind* of poet they exalted while deploring his way of life. . . . If there is more fiction in it than I know, I should like to be set right; in some instances, which I shall call attention to later, my memory has already been corrected.
>
> One great handicap to this task of recalling has been the fact of being an orphan. The chain of recollection—the collective memory of a family—has been broken. It is our parents, normally, who not only teach us our family history but who set us straight on our own childhood recollections, telling us that *this* cannot have happened the way we think it did and that *that*, on the other hand, did occur, just as we remember it. (pp. 4–5)

Orphanhood also produces an urgency about retrieving personal history, which McCarthy notices in herself and in her brothers. In reconstructing their history they debate the details available from family photos, compare stories that seem incomplete or improbable, challenge information—such as the rumor their father was alcoholic—with childhood's "truth test": "I am as certain as I can be that my father did not drink when I was a little girl. Children are sensitive to such things; their sense of smell, first of all, seems sharper than other people's, and they do not like the smell of alcohol" (p. 14).

McCarthy also tells us why she emphasizes the *Catholic* girlhood in her title, for not only does it underscore some of the rigidity of her guardian's behavior, but it is also the avenue for aesthetic escape that the young, creative sensibility she recollects requires.

> Looking back, I see that it was religion that saved me. Our ugly church and parochial school provided me with my only aesthetic outlet, in the words of the Mass and the litanies and the old Latin hymns, in the Easter lilies around the altar, rosaries, ornamented prayer books, votive lamps, holy cards stamped in gold and decorated with flower wreaths and a saint's picture. This side of Catholicism, much of it cheapened and debased by mass production, was for me, nevertheless, the equivalent of Gothic cathedrals and illuminated manuscripts and mystery plays. I threw myself into it with ardor. (p. 26)

The story that McCarthy relates is one of losing her parents to the great influenza epidemic of 1918, having her paternal grandparents assume guardianship, and then being assigned to the care of a great aunt, Margaret, who with her authoritarian husband, Meyers Shriver, forced the children to live in harsh and barren conditions. The sense of abandonment, rejection, and emotional sterility that the guardianship fostered is recreated in the vignettes, and then re-examined in the voice-overs. After a chapter on convent life, for example, she assesses: "This story is so true to our convent life that I find it almost impossible to sort out the guessed-at and the half-remembered from the undeniably real" (p. 124). Or after an account of a conversation with the Mother Superior of her boarding school registering concern for "her grandfather's soul," she observes, "this account is highly fictionalized" (p. 99).

McCarthy's very acknowledgment of the intersection of fiction and fact creates the verisimilitude of *Memories of a Catholic Girlhood*. By constantly reminding the reader of the way memory adjusts history, or children's needs color an event with a particular hue, McCarthy convinces us to trust her record. She, like Hellman, pulls the reader into empathetic engagement precisely because she alerts the reader to its dangers.

McCarthy emphasizes the "ambiguity of a fiction writer turned autobiographer" (Eakin, 1985, p. 10) by launching her own investigation into how an established writer of fiction assembles a series of sketches about the self and binds them into "memoirs." McCarthy was, in fact, a well-known writer of short stories when the first sketches for *Girlhood* began to appear in *The New Yorker* in 1944. Eight of these pieces eventually appeared, and 13 years later she presented them in the single volume, *Memories of a Catholic Girlhood*.

May Sarton duplicates this process with *I Knew a Phoenix: Sketches for an Autobiography*. *The New Yorker* published sections of these "sketches" in 1956, 1957, and 1958, apparently as part of a larger autobiography still awaiting completion. As she said in a 1987 interview I conducted at her York, Maine home, "Norton wants me to write a [complete] autobiography. But I can't look back. Not now. I have more life to live." What prompted her to "look back" in her mid-40s? And how did she select pivotal moments or key people as vehicles for vivifying her early years?

For Sarton, the impetus for the writing of her first autobiographical volume was two-pronged. First, by her mid-40s she had amassed considerable experience with a rich European literary culture—one that included the Huxleys, Virginia and Leonard Woolf, Elizabeth Bowen—writers who beg to be written about. Second, she was assessing an important chapter in her artistic life. *I Knew a Phoenix* chronicles her early success and failure in Eva La Galienne's Civic Repertory Theatre, her later efforts to succeed with the Apprentice Theatre, and finally her shift to the metier she sees as her primary one: poetry. As she closes the door on theatre, she opens another "into the intensities of the private life, of time, of solitude, of poetry" (p. 196).

The volume is triggered by a psychological turning point as well as a vocational one. Sarton does not reveal many of these experiences until 20 years after they occur. Her internal clock registers the need to commit these portraits to paper as she is passing from one phase of her artistic life to another, as she feels herself standing alone, a kind of "orphan." Her need to record her childhood, the emotional and psychological "loam" in which she was nurtured, parallels the impulses present in Hellman and McCarthy, just as her sense of orphanhood lends urgency to the assessments of her parents.

The first portraits in *I Knew a Phoenix* are of Sarton's extraordinary parents, who, for all their artistic and intellectual gifts, thought of themselves as "exiles." She records their painful exit from war-torn Belgium in 1915 and their nomadic early years in America. Eventually George Sarton, who became internationally famous for his multivolumed scholarly *History of Science*, settled at Harvard. But still they felt, as Sarton put it later, "very little sense of community," and Sarton's office where he put in an 8-hour work day was a tiny room in Widener Library. "We were exiles, no doubt," Sarton says and in *Phoenix* she recalls being displayed by well-meaning associates as a "refugee." Given this sense of displacement, it is not surprising that Sarton's highest praise is accorded to those who "make me feel at home, at least for a time."

The need to root, to connect meaningfully to a tradition, a house, a garden, a sense of community, is deeply felt in Sarton's portrait of her father, a man iron-willed in scholarly detachment who longs for wife and family so he "will no longer be alone." The need for roots registers more subtly in the portrait of Mabel Elwes, Sarton's mother, twice transplanted, from England to Belgium to America, yet always striving to create a sense of "home" for her husband and child. Its most resounding echo is in Sarton herself, the only child of brilliant parents, uprooted at 3 from Belgium, vacillating between Europe and America during her formative years, gradually recognizing that her path to a "community" would be through her art and that her extended family would be her audience.

Seen in this light, *I Knew a Phoenix* opens a window on Sarton's sense of what friends and shaping influences lessened her sense of exile, providing her with a "community." Although she may be "adopted" by friends and mentors temporarily, she gradually comes to accept that a commitment to art exacts a heavy tribute in isolation. Solitude is what the artist craves, not isolation; she characterizes the first as a condition in which one experiences richness of the self, and the second as a loneliness where one grinds along in the poverty of the self.

Shortly after *I Knew a Phoenix* was published, George and Mabel Sarton died; May Sarton left the home she shared with Judy Matlack for 12 years in Cambridge and began a new phase in her career, establishing a residence first in Nelson, New Hampshire and later in York, Maine, where she works as a poet, novelist, and keeper of journals that celebrate the joys and rigors of "a life of solitude." *I Knew a Phoenix* marks the point where old fears of orphanhood succumb to the new challenges of solitude.

I Knew a Phoenix demonstrates, perhaps more transparently than any of the other autobiographical writings discussed in this chapter, the struggle of the female writer to achieve autonomy *and* attachment. And since childhood patterns are replayed throughout the individual's life, the reader is looking at a past very much alive in present consciousness.

Paul John Eakin has usefully summarized recent theory regarding a variety of "pacts between reader and author" that aid in understanding how autobiography is a necessary consequence of the writer's *present* consciousness (*Fictions in Autobiography*, pp. 20ff). Philippe Lejeune, he says, theorizes about author's "intention," suggesting that autobiographical texts, explicitly or implicitly, create "a pact between author and reader" (p. 20). Lejeune's view is confirmed in part by Norman Holland and Elizabeth Bruss, who detail the kinds of expectations an autobiographical text triggers in readers. But it is particularly in the work of James Olney (*Metaphors of Self: The Meaning of Autobiography*, 1972) that Eakin locates the shift from autobiography as verifiable, historic past to autobiography as a function of the author's *present consciousness*. Olney construes the autobiographical act as "a monument of the self as it is becoming, a metaphor of the self at the summary moment of composition." Thus, concludes Eakin, "if autobiographical texts do not tell us as much about the autobiographer's past history as earlier students of the genre wished to believe, they may nevertheless . . . tell us about the autobiographer in the moment . . . of composition" (Eakin, p. 22).

Seen in this light, the "portraits of the past" by Gornick, Chernin, Steinem, McCarthy, Hellman, and Sarton illumine the ongoing literary history in which they are, as writers, engaged. Their portraits (although they include fathers, guardians, nuns, significant peers) reveal valuable insights about the nurturance of mother figures and the quality of emotional life that runs in tandem with their art.

Angelou, Walker, and Kingston add another layer to the mix: Their stories foregrounding powerful mothers are also signified by markers of race and ethnicity, markers they must decode for themselves and for readers who may find themselves in unfamiliar territory. Minority autobiography, as Nellie McKay (1988), Susan Stanford Friedman (1988), William Andrews (1986), Stephen Butterfield (1974), and Elizabeth Fox-Genovese (1987) have all pointed out, depends on some sense of "community identity." Identity within the minority culture helps individuals move beyond the alienation present in the dominant culture. Some "authentic self" results *in relation* to the ethnic community whether that self is forged in competition with or in fusion with the values the community expresses.

If the reader accepts the autobiographical act as a function of a writer's present consciousness, one steeped in a particular time, set of circumstances, ethnic and cultural mix, then several repeating emphases resonate from the juxtaposed "nurturance stories" of Gornick, Chernin, Angelou, Walker, Steinem, McCarthy, Hellman, Sarton, and Kingston. Whether cast as a biological mother, grandmother, personal mentor, or Catholic *mater dolorosa*, the burgeoning female self feels she owes loyalty, allegiance, and accountability to the "mother"; at the same time she recognizes that those very allegiances threaten, overshadow, or imperil her own life and art. While some fathers or male mentors are seen sympathetically or even admiringly (Sarton's father, Hellman's lover, Angelou's brother), the worlds in which the young woman matures are intensely female. Male worlds remain private, authoritarian rather than transformative.

A second emphasis is the act of "breaking silence." Several of the authors suffer physiological muteness (Angelou, Kingston); more commonly the authors describe psychological or emotional barriers to speech: these include the censorship of guilt (Gornick, Chernin), the repression of shame (Steinem, Kingston), the alienation of orphanhood or exile (Sarton, McCarthy, Hellman). The female autobiographer deploys language to convey the feeling of being cut off from language. In the absence of verifying parents, she creates a narrative, allowing her to "parent" herself. All are professional wordsmiths, yet their own childhood stories document struggles with articulation.

The third emphasis is the consciousness of a collaborative reader. Whether invited in directly (as in Steinem's opening paragraph in "Ruth's Song") or indirectly (as in Walker's exfoliation of the symbol of her "mother's gardens"), the female autobiographies demonstrate an awareness of and, to a greater or lesser extent, a responsibility for an engaged reader—one who is granted permission to use the story as *exemplum*.

In an atmosphere crackling with the indictments of Dinnerstein, sensitized by the passionate persuasion of Rich, instructed by the careful psychological constructs of Miller, readers of female autobiographies are well prepared to engage in "crucial conversations," ones that sought to reexamine the roles of primary "caregiver," "daughter," "artist."

Notes

1 There are many useful volumes tracing the influence of new cognitive models and developmental theory over the course of the past 25 years. Among those most instructive are Jay R. Greenberg and Stephen A. Mitchell, *Object Relations in Psychoanalytic Theory* (Cambridge, MA, Harvard University Press: 1983); *Women's Ways of Knowing: The Development of Self, Voice, and Mind*, Belenky, Clinchy, Goldberger, Tarule, eds. (New York, Basic Books: 1986); *Women's Growth in Connection: Writings from the Stone Center*, Jordan et al., eds. (New York, Guilford Press: 1991); and Nancy Chodorow, *Feminism and Psychoanalytic Theory* (New Haven, Yale University Press: 1989).

2 As quoted in Janet Surrey, "The Self-in-Relation: A Theory of Women's Development," *Women's Growth in Connection: Writings from the Stone Center*, p. 57. Chodorow's results have been criticized because of her omission of class and race distinctions, just as Gilligan's theories of moral development have been contested by those who argue that male/female oppositional thinking collapses "differences" simply into gender categories. I'm interested less in "essentialist" vs. "pluralist" arguments than in the patterns evident in the texts themselves. For more detailed discussions of "difference" in Chodorow, see Linda Nicholson and

Nancy Fraser, "Social Criticism Without Philosophy: An Encounter Between Feminism and Postmodernism," in *Postmodernism/Feminism*, Linda Nicholson, ed. (London, Routledge: 1990, pp. 19–38).

3 Recent statistics indicate that 26% of the population in the United States live in what is considered the "traditional nuclear family"; 62% of infants under one year of age have mothers in the workforce; 87% of all children are being raised by multiple caregivers rather than one primary caregiver (cited in public lecture, Patricia Hertz, Smith School for Social Work, July 1992).

◆ 2 ◆

Memory and Metaphor

> We do "live again" in memory . . . in history as well as in biography. And when these two come together, forming a narrative, they approach fiction. The imprecision of memory causes us to create, to extend remembrance into narrative. It sometimes seems, therefore, that what we remember is not—could not be—true. And yet it is *accurate*. The imagination, triggered by memory, is satisfied that this is so.
> —Patricia Hampl, *A Romantic Education*

Memory, Lillian Hellman tells us, is a slippery thing. It can blur the specific detail in order to recover the generic truth; it can group events and reorder them so as to demonstrate exfoliating meaning; it can invest the tumble of the spontaneous or accidental with the wisdom of hindsight. As May Sarton suggests, artists make myths of their lives in order to sustain hope, cut losses, negotiate pain. And as Patricia Hampl adds, in *A Romantic Education* (1981), memories of childhood are marinated in appropriate bits of what we've read or heard since then and what we *choose* to believe. We see the past, in female autobiography, in something of the same way we see a Henry Moore sculpture. The "holes" define the "shape." What is left repressed, or what cannot be uttered, is often as significant to the whole shape of the life as what is said.

> We trust memory against all the evidence: it is selective, subjective, cannily defensive, unreliable as fact. But a single red detail remembered—a hat worn in 1952, the nail polish applied one summer day by an aunt to her toes, separated by balls of cotton, as we watched—has more real blood than the creatures around us on a bus as, for some reason, we think of that day, that hat, those bright feet. That world. This power of memory probably comes from its kinship with the imagination. (p. 5)

Myth-Making: Reconstructing the Past

How memory, with all of its built-in biases and special needs, yokes with the imagination—often through the medium of metaphor—to discover or create the "felt truth" of a particular life experience is the focus of this chapter. Always an autobiographer's struggle, the task of "naming and claiming" the truths of life experience is exacerbated for the female autobiographer for reasons I will also explore.

May Sarton engages that struggle in *A World of Light*. Written in 1976, it involves some of the same people as *I Knew a Phoenix*. She attempts to portray influential figures in her life "against the backdrop of their time and culture." Sarton suggests that she first conceived of the book as resembling "the Renaissance portraits where the subject is painted with the landscape behind him, a landscape that is very much a part of the character and the mood of the portrait" (p. 15). In some instances she finds a very telling connection between person and place, and when that relationship serves to illumine the life, she employs it.

But almost immediately, Sarton speaks of conflicts she experiences in reconstructing the past, conflicts that display her awareness of multiple selves within the first person "I" and her own needs, "startling truths . . . that have helped me understand myself" (p. 16). She tries to create the "I" as it functioned in the past while at the same time finding its contours instructive in the present.

> Nothing in the past stays fixed forever; as we grow and change the past changes; when I look back I did not always find exactly what I had expected, and even such seminal friendships became mine fields. (p. 15)

She struggles with mechanisms that capture the past both as it happened and simultaneously suggest its flux. "How to pin down even a small part of the truth? . . . How to find the balance between the essence of a person and our relationship?" (p. 23). Usually the essence of a person is available to her via some aspect of her relationship with them. Hence, her portraits are intimate in tone, relational in method, and suggest that assessment is measured in terms of personal impact. They employ metaphor as a poet might, substituting for "factual data" a suggestive image that catches the "essence" of the person.

As in *I Knew a Phoenix*, Sarton's first portraits are of her parents. Admitting in her introduction that she has omitted any explanation of "what it was like to be their child," Sarton tries to see her parents animated by their daily habits. George Sarton, a man entirely and almost obsessively devoted to creating a new discipline, the *History of Science*, is portrayed as one "whose work took precedence over everything else." He was "a man bent over a desk in a tiny book filled study in the Widener Library at Harvard University for many hours each day, whose image of himself was that of a crusader in a holy war" (p. 28).

His love of scholarship, which prompted him to found the first national journal for the history of science, to learn Arabic "for the sake of his
medieval studies" (p. 29), and to spend Saturday afternoons "at the Museum of Arts in Boston, studying Chinese painting for the sheer pleasure
of it," often foreclosed other possibilities for easy give-and-take in the
family. George Sarton took no interest in money, often leaving the man-
agement of a scanty salary to his wife as well as abdicating all responsibility for the care of young May.

Sarton's reconstruction of her father's life, his passion and reserve,
his daily regimen, his needs and fears, derives much of its detail from his
journals. Not only does this technique serve to order the information she
reports, but it also reinforces the conclusions she draws from a number of
quoted entries.

Mabel Sarton, artist, twice transplanted emigre (England to Belgium;
Belgium to America) is less clearly rendered in Sarton's portrait, perhaps
because her personality was subsumed by the towering needs of her husband. The thwarting of her own talent, the loneliness of a wife whose
husband works 18 hours a day for a lifetime, the internalized frustration
she must have felt as a consequence of his behavior are all documented as
part of the dynamic of the Sarton marriage.

> My mother never made scenes. She buried her anger, because, how-
> ever angry she was—and with reason—she still felt that George Sarton must
> be protected, never upset by any demands of hers, for the sake of his work.
> The cost was high, high in ill health, migraine, and I have sometimes won-
> dered whether the cancer of which she died might not have been caused by
> buried rage. (p. 19)

Her love of gardening, seemingly inexhaustible and a lifelong passion,
provides the vehicle by which Sarton tries to capture her essence.

> Sometimes seed catalogues were the avenue to an early morning ex-
> cursion. What if she had ten dollars to spend? Would it be for English as-
> ters? Lilies? Iris? Imaginary gardens flowered in her head.
> By six she and Cloudy [her cat] were ready to go out to taste the morn-
> ing and do some work in the real garden. So by the time most of the world
> was just waking up, she had already lived the most intense and rewarding
> hours of her day. People thought of my mother as frail—and in fact she rarely
> felt well—but when I think of what she asked of herself in an average day
> when she was past seventy, I see her as a fountain of energy, flowing up in
> a sparkling plume, then dying down gradually. (pp. 50–51)

Sarton does not specify just how either of her parents directly affected
her life (except to say she tries to be as dedicated a worker as her father

and as humane a person as her mother), nor does she correlate the dynamic of their marriage to her own "rage" and courage. Still we feel, in what Lacan would call its "absence," the presence of Sarton's "self" and the influencing forces upon it. She confesses that after they both died she felt a sense of relief—"freed from the great burden of being a child . . . I also felt a new responsibility, since a person without any family can afford to be honest in a way that perhaps no one with any close ties can be" (p. 22).

After the portraits of her parents Sarton includes two sections of accounts of people once vital to her development: Celine Dangotte Limbosch, a childhood friend of her mother's in school at Ghent and a kind of "nanny" to the young Sarton; Edith Forbes Kennedy, a surrogate mother for Sarton in her early artistic experiments in Cambridge and Paris; Grace Eliot Dudley in her French retreat near the village of Vouvray; Alice and Hamel Long who befriended Sarton on a poetry reading stop at Santa Fe. These sections end with two portraits of "uncommon commoners": Marc Turian, a Swiss vigneron, and Albert Quigley, a painter and fiddle player who farmed not far from Sarton's Nelson, New Hampshire home for 15 years. Although these may seem like cameo appearances (they reappear in Sarton's journals in much fuller detail), each represents an "authentic I" impacting powerfully on Sarton's development as a person and as a writer, and both are caught in some characteristic posture or activity.

The fourth section is devoted to more well-known figures. The individuals described here—S.S. Koteliansky, Elizabeth Bowen, and Louise Bogan—take their vitality and animation from the love Sarton feels for them. In each instance they are described juxtaposed with Sarton: "Kot" in his kitchen, Bowen as an overnight visitor in Sarton's studio, Bogan as an honored guest to "warm" Sarton's first home in Nelson, New Hampshire.

In portraits of S.S. Koteliansky, Elizabeth Bowen, and Louise Bogan, Sarton is most clearly the "memoirist," reconstructing and illuminating each subject from memory. Not only do we feel the presence of Bowen's Anglo-Irish intensity, Bogan's keen and acidic wit, Kot's "spiritual grit," but also how Sarton vibrated to their impact and energy. She captures the force of "the other" on a young, somewhat tentative but always daring "self." However, she seems acutely aware of her own needs in each relationship and dares to name her loves and errors even when the cost is great. For example, she says this about her attraction to Bowen:

> I understood that earlier in her life she had loved at least one woman
> but I gathered that that period was over. Now her love affairs were with men.
> She seemed to take it quite naturally that she could be in love and still very
> much married to Alan. I was at that time bursting out of a puritan envelope,

and all this amazed, touched, shook, and filled me with love for this extraordinary woman who could be at the same time so open and so grand, so much a genius and so human, and above all, as vulnerable as I was, apparently, to sudden irrational attachments. (p. 196)

For Sarton, studying the vitality of Elizabeth Bowen's attachments allows her to understand her own and frees her to explore her own needs and network of influence.

If, as Sarton suggests, "landscape is very much a part of the character and mood of the portrait," part of her method in *A World of Light* is to suggest the metaphoric relationship between a particular setting and the subject who inhabits it. Some of the most vivid passages in the volume are of locations, settings for the creative act. Her mother's flourishing garden, her father's tiny office in Widener Library, Koteliansky's warm, scrubbed kitchen, Louise Bogan's peacock blue and gray apartment—all function as more than physical places. They contain an *animus* of their own, bearing a kind of reciprocity with their creators. When Sarton describes the details of such a setting, she drops a deep vertical shaft of light into the artist who inhabits it. Here, for example, is her description of S.S. Koteliansky's house at 5 Acadia Road, where Katherine Mansfield once lived.

> The four rooms where Kot lived contained, as I have suggested, a minimum of furniture, and this of the plainest. There was no "easy" chair, for instance; there were not many books, but these, the essential, notably all the Russian classics. It was kept so immaculate by Kot himself, with the help of a weekly char, that every floor shone and a speck of dust would have been a sacrilege. Upstairs in the front room there was a painting by his old friend Beatrice Cambell of Kot and Katherine Mansfield sitting in deck chairs in the garden; there was a table with books and papers on it, a jar of pencils, and a little green bowl given to him by K.M.; there were two or three straight chairs, a radio and a bookcase. Here Kot often sat in the evening watching the light fade and listening to the news. He slept in the monastic back room. Belowstairs there was a dining room, never used, opening through French doors into the garden, of which he was proud because, although he himself did little work there, each plant and flower had been put in by a friend and so had become an extension of the lares and penates inside. But the center of his life was the warm, sunny kitchen, which he reached each day like an island, after making his bed, having breakfast and washing the dishes at a dark sink down the hall. Here in the kitchen he could busy himself with the real things—books and friends. (pp. 177–178)

In creating an emotional context as well as a physical setting, she takes the reader down through the strata, exposing salient details about the subject in each successive "layer."

The measure of the person is, to a large extent in *A World of Light*, calibrated to his or her impact on Sarton—a method that escapes egotism by its very self-consciousness. It is a method also echoing Nancy Chodorow's contention that female identity is defined through attachment. And if, as Carol Gilligan argues, women experience moral choices as arising from "webs of connection," Sarton's final picture of Kot is surely meant as a tribute to his integrity and moral fiber.

> . . . as I think back to the warm tiny kitchen where we talked so often and so long, I realize that there is no room in the world where I have ever felt so absolutely at home, if being at home means being comfortable spiritually, being able to be completely myself without fear or embarrassment because I was sitting opposite an old man who was completely himself and who was not afraid of a rather high emotional temperature—in fact, thrived on it. (p. 188)

Autobiographical truth revealed through memory and metaphor is not the same as historical truth; the autobiographical act is simultaneously an invention and a discovery: It must, as Sarton's work suggests, be seen in its own context as the product of the felt needs of its creator. No one has demonstrated that more powerfully in the late twentieth century or paid a higher price for it than Lillian Hellman.

Pentimento (1973) and *Scoundrel Time* (1976) display the autobiographical mode Hellman experimented with but did not perfect in *An Unfinished Woman*: portraits. *Pentimento*, subtitled *A Book of Portraits*, contains seven organically shaped profiles of people Hellman loved. There is little effort to sustain a chronological narrative throughout, although, as with Sarton, there is some historical overlapping and a sense of chronological progression. And like Sarton, Hellman, although visible, keeps herself in the background, suggesting her responses indirectly, creating a self-portrait that is impressionistic and psychologically elliptical. Even when, as in *Scoundrel Time*, she concentrates on one historical event—her appearance before the House Un-American Activities Committee in 1952—she deliberately breaks the unified narrative flow by alluding to events as early as 1929 and as late as 1975, melding diary notes with current reflections.

Each portrait represents a major player in either Hellman's life or her emotional development, a force that helps her struggle for self-definition and for an accurate portrayal of the historical forces at work in her time. She plumbs her childhood both for what was sustaining and for what sabotaged an adult sense of self-esteem and stability of temperament. Sophronia, her black nanny and confidante of a childhood split between New York and New Orleans, she characterizes as "the anchor for a little girl." Yet simultaneously she senses Sophronia's vulnerability—the consequence of class, sex, and color.

In her memories of "Bethe" and "Willy" Hellman describes intense feelings prompted by a German woman brought to this country to marry a cousin and by Uncle Willy, who runs guns to South America to quell disturbances by disobedient blacks. In both instances, Hellman struggles with the conflict between what she ought to feel—loyalty to the family in the face of Bethe's taking a Mafia lover, and contempt for Uncle Willy because of her love for Sophronia—and the acknowledged "perverse thrill" she feels for both risk-takers. Looking back on these experiences in *Pentimento*, with the perspective of the present, she writes:

> There are many ways of falling in love and one seldom is more interesting or valid than another. . . . I was not ever to fall in love very often, but certainly this was the first time and I would like to think I learned from it. But the mixture of ecstasy as it clashed with criticism of myself and the man was to be repeated all my life, and the only thing that made the feeling for Uncle Willy different was the pain of that first recognition: not of love, but of the struggles caused by love; the blindness of a young girl trying to make simple sexual desire into something more complex, more poetic, more unreadable. (p. 61)

As she moves into her adult years, she writes once again about Dashiell Hammett, the figure she celebrated in *An Unfinished Woman* and whose presence is also keenly felt in *Scoundrel Time*. She avoids direct characterization of their relationship, although they lived together off and on for some 30 years. Her restraint in describing her feelings for Hammett mimics his Hemingwayesque style and serves to intensify their relationship. The two concluding chapters of *Pentimento* explore the nature of that relationship, its explosions, and its remarkable staying power. Both circle around the question of confronting and accepting death, at first metaphorically and then literally. In "Turtle" Hammett and Hellman capture and behead a snapping turtle menacing their lake—the next morning they discover that the decapitated body has mysteriously moved itself from the kitchen to the brush outside. Hammett wants to retrieve it for soup; Hellman resists.

> "Let's take it to the lake. It's earned its life."
> "It's dead. It's been dead since yesterday."
> "No. Or maybe it was dead and now it isn't." (p. 229)

Finally, she asks him to bury the turtle.

> "I don't bury turtles."
> "Will you bury me?"
> "When the time comes, I'll do my best," he said. (pp. 232–233)

But it's Hellman who performs Hammett's burial and in "Pentimento," the final sketch describes the slow and gradual process of coming to terms with Hammett's death. Her explanation pivots on her use of the term "Pentimento"—since she defines memory as "seeing and then seeing again" (p. 1).

> Old paint, on canvas, as it ages, sometimes becomes transparent. When that happens it is possible, in some pictures, to see the original lines: a tree will show through a woman's dress, a child makes way for a dog, a large boat is no longer on an open sea. That is called pentimento, because the painter "repented," changed his mind. Perhaps it would be as well to say that the old conception, replaced by the later choice, is a way of seeing and then seeing again.
>
> That is all I mean about the people in this book. The paint has aged now and I wanted to see what was there for me once, what is there for me now. (p. 1)

The most controversial segments in these portraits concern the depiction of Hellman's political conscience, caught most memorably in the now infamous "Julia" episode. In "Julia" Hellman describes a trip across Germany in 1937 to deliver $50,000 in ransom money to a childhood friend, code-named Julia, who in turn will funnel it into efforts to free political prisoners of the Nazis. Hellman's account concentrates on the train ride and her mounting panic over the possibility of discovery, registering bits and pieces of information about Julia via flashback. These include Julia's relinquishment of her inheritance to work for the underground, a 1934 meeting in a Viennese hospital where Julia was recuperating from a leg amputation, and attempts to locate a child Julia bore and sent to London for safety—all segments that develop the reader's sympathy for the heroic Julia and her stalwart friend, Lillian.

Hellman's self-deprecating tone downplays her own role, emphasizing her fear and the staggering ineptitude of carelessly leaving the hat into which the ransom money is sewed lying on a seat when she leaves her compartment momentarily. The effect of the memoir is to cast Hellman as an unlikely but thoroughly admirable freedom fighter. (The book was a best-seller, enthusiastically reviewed, and turned into a film with the Julia episode starring Vanessa Redgrave and Jane Fonda.)

Scoundrel Time, Hellman's angry recollections of the 1950s, focuses on the "Red Scare" after World War II, caught poignantly in the moment of Hammett's refusal to testify about a bail bond fund of the Civil Rights Congress of which he was a trustee, a gesture that resulted in his 1951 incarceration. At the center of what she terms "my own history of the time" is her appearance before the House Un-American Activities Committee hearings in 1952. The actual hearing is recorded in only six pages, while another 120 are devoted to building tension before the hearing and collected anecdotes about those she vilifies after the hearing. She specifically indicts those intellectuals and liberals, some of whom were still alive in 1976, who betrayed friends and disavowed political ideas: Harry Cohn, who wanted her to sign a million dollar contract requiring a loyalty oath; Clifford Odets, who bragged about loyalty to friends, then turned friendly witness on the stand; Henry Wallace, who betrayed the very communists who supported his Progressive Party. Essentially *Scoundrel Time* is neither ideological nor historical. At heart, it is a personal meditation—wry, ironic, idiosyncratic—and it is precisely Hellman's angling and perhaps doctoring of factual truth, in the service of creating "a personal truth," that puts her at the center of a heated debate for the remainder of her lifetime. To her admirers she is the example *par excellence* of tough-minded integrity during a "scoundrel time" in American history. To her detractors she is a self-aggrandizing liar who invented Julia and her own anti-McCarthy activity to snooker the public and promote herself as the "conscience for a corrupt era." By the time of her death in 1984, Hellman had an "enemies list as long as Richard Nixon's," as Frank Rich wrote in *The New York Times Book Review*, and many liberals were on it: Elizabeth Hardwick, Irving Howe, Alfred Kazin, Diana Trilling, and Mary McCarthy. It was McCarthy who provoked Hellman into bringing a two million dollar libel suit, by telling the TV interviewer Dick Cavett in 1980 that "every word" Hellman wrote was "a lie, including 'and' and 'the.'" The veracity of Hellman's memoirs is an interesting case that her biographer, William Wright (*Lillian Hellman, the Image, the Woman*, 1986) has objectively unfolded. His research leaves little doubt that the pseudonymous "Julia" was Muriel Gardiner— a woman Hellman neither knew firsthand nor assisted in heroic anti-Nazi activities. While there is little doubt that Hellman "suffered badly" as a consequence of the McCarthy blacklist, Wright's research also pulls the rug from under the implication that she had to sell her Westchester farm because of the financial hardships resulting from the blacklist.

Surely at the heart of this controversy is the question of what constitutes autobiographical truth and the even thornier question of what we *expect* it to be. On the one hand, Hellman deliberately avoided documentary or claims of historical accuracy by suggesting the metaphor of "Pentimento," "seeing old paint behind new on a canvas," and by claiming to write "my history of the '50s." Should she be judged by how deftly and engaging she is in evoking "portraits," the temper of the times, a feel of a particular brand of totalitarianism? Or does such a record in the act of *persuading the reader of its verisimilitude* require absolute historical accuracy and factual precision? Perhaps the reason "untruth" is such a serious matter in Hellman's case is that she herself casts hard judgments on prominent figures and governmental authorities who shade or shape "the truth" by a hundred imprecisions. Does she fail by her own standards? Or is she perhaps in some unconscious way revealing the "emotional truth" of the 1950s antihero, always hedging bets, manipulating facts, practicing self-protection?

The Julia controversy in *Pentimento* also highlights autobiography's power to act as "moral example" (Jane Marcus's phrase), satisfying some expectation of what we believe the truth to be. The reader who has identified with the inept, self-deprecating Hellman of *Pentimento* and *Scoundrel Time* feels betrayed by evidence that she may have invented versions of a narrative designed to make her look heroic. As a student in an undergraduate seminar on autobiography said upon making this discovery: "She duped me. I can't forgive her for betraying my trust." Hellman's narratives convinced, and since they explored moral questions, a reader's "trust" is precisely what was manipulated. Yet her portraits, "fictional" (or dramatic) as they may be, catch the "essence" of the times in ways documentary might not.

At issue is the elusive border that separates imagination from truth and, as documentarist film maker Errol Morris has observed, "our need to believe what we want to believe is a lot stronger than our need to seek the truth." Hellman's dominant discourse convinces us of the veracity of her account; yet when we understand the function of (selective) memory and (representational) metaphor, we are aware of a *constructed* reality, one that we and the author are making "real." In a pact with Hellman, we substitute her account for reality.[1]

William Wright offers this respectful if speculative scene in the last pages of his biography, *Lillian Hellman, the Image, the Woman*:

> The picture of Hellman alone at her typewriter, writing her memoirs, is haunting. The disparate motives that surely struggled within her to write a gripping tale, to be admired, to settle scores, to justify herself, to write out the pain and humiliation—all of those could have come to supersede the impulse to present an accurate record. She might have felt that not only the blank pages were "wanting" but so her history, if only in her own eyes. *Perhaps* she approached the task with her well-trained dramatist's eye and sought to create a character that "worked." And sitting in that creative posture—weighing what to include, what to omit—the temptation to break loose from the confining truth may have been too great to resist. And she may have lost the ability to distinguish between what she had been and what she wished she had been. (p. 434)

Memory yielding a better version of reality than what transpired, is part of what Patricia Hampl explores in *A Romantic Education*. Memory, for

Hampl, contains within it both historical and emotional accuracy, getting closer to what happened, why, and its ultimate significance than documentary ever can. But its primary purpose is to clarify, never falsify. It does not report life per se but creates a life of its own on the page that clarifies the life as lived.

> The self-absorption that seems to be the impetus and embarrassment of autobiography turns into (or perhaps always was) a hunger for the world. Actually, it begins as hunger for *a* world, one gone or lost, effaced by time or a more sudden brutality. But in the act of remembering, the personal environment expands, resonates beyond itself, beyond its "subject" into the endless and tragic recollection that is history.
>
> We look back at old family photographs in which we stand next to black, boxy Fords and are wearing period costumes, and we do not gaze fascinated because there we are so young again, or there we are standing, as we will never again in life, next to our mother. . . . It is the dress, the black car that dazzle us now and draw us beyond our mother's bright arms which once caught us. We reach into the attractive impersonality of something more significant than ourselves. (p. 5)

"Something more significant than ourselves" is created by memory's kinship to imagination. That memory is simply retrieval and the job of the memoirist simply transcription, Hampl disputes in her essay "Memory and Imagination." "No memoirist writes for long without experiencing an unsettling belief about the reliability of memory, a hunch that memory is not, after all, *just* memory (emphasis added)" (p. 695). Hampl suggests that the memoirist writes not out of the impulse to relay to the reader what she already knows but, *in the act of telling*, to discover what she has come to know. "Intentionality" doesn't "run the show," says Hampl, "the heart, the guardian of intuition with its secret, often fearful intentions, is the boss. Its commands are what a writer obeys—often without knowing it" (p. 697). A reader has a "right to expect a memoir to be as accurate as the writer's memory can make it" (p. 698). But lies don't hamper the memoirist as much as misdirections in the "real subject" (p. 698), the raison d'etre of the essay.

Hampl suggests that the "accuracy" of an autobiographical piece depends on its correlation to the real subject, conveying to the reader its substance through detail and metaphor. What the autobiographical writer must do is select from the warehouse of stored experience those images and details that bear congruence with the real subject. "Stalking the relationship, seeking the congruence between stored image and hidden image—that's the real job of memoir" (p. 698).

When those details correlate to the real subject, "memory reaches out its arms and embraces imagination" (p. 699). It is here that the reader finds entry, where personal truth (via image and symbol grown transpersonal) escapes the specific instances that give rise to it and enlarges to universal conditions. Hampl sees in this enlarged meaning the authentic impulse to write autobiography.

> We wish to talk to each other about life and death, about love, despair, loss, and innocence. We sense that in order to live together we must learn to speak of peace, of history, of meaning and values.
> We see a means of exchange, a language which will renew these ancient concerns and make them wholly and pulsingly ours. Instinctively, we go to our store of private images and associations for our authority. (pp. 699–700)

The peculiar appeal of the memoir to the reader, as Hampl sees it, is the drive that prompts us all to create our versions of the past, to sift our experience for the essential grain—or to locate in its chaff what we have purposefully or intuitively discarded or devaluated. It also lies in the drive to tell our own stories and then to listen to what they mean. Herein lies her startling linkage to Sarton's notion of a Renaissance painter's use of background and to Hellman's notion of "Pentimento." "To write one's life is to live it twice," says Hampl, "the first time as a 'tourist,' the second time as a 'pilgrim'." And to publish one's story is to extend its received meanings in a third resignification to the reader.

A Romantic Education is the story of Hampl's midwestern childhood; of her coming of age in the 1960s in a climate of political protest; and of her journey to the "golden Prague" of her family's past.

Born to a family who is "crazy about the past," Hampl starts her memoir in St. Paul, Minnesota in her grandmother's house, where she is entertaining herself by leafing through a book of sepia photos of "Golden Prague, Views of the Nineteenth Century" (p. 3). Her grandmother appears in the doorway to call the child to dinner and upon seeing her interest in the album, sinks to the floor with her, absorbed in the photos, dabbing at her face behind her "foreign eyeglasses," murmuring, "So beautiful. So beautiful."

St. Paul is beautiful too, as Hampl recollects it, Scott Fitzgerald's city, the city of rivers, the city of immigrants, of warm Catholic neighborhoods, a city of glowing street lights, a *romantic* city. Even the relentless winter was defined as a symptom of beauty.

> The cold was our pride, the snow was our beauty. It fell and fell, lacing day and night together in a milky haze, making everything quieter as it fell, so that winter seemed to partake of religion in a way no other season did, hushed, solemn. It was snowing and it was silent. Good-bye, good-bye, we are leaving you forever: this was the farewell we sent to the nation on the *Today Show* weather report. (p. 52)

The inwardness of eternal winters, the example of the lush romantic yearnings of Scott Fitzgerald's childhood, the romance of street lights worthy "of Chekhov" inspire Hampl to contemplate the nature and resourcefulness of "Beauty," the subject of the middle section bridging the St. Paul and Prague sections of *A Romantic Education*. Beauty has more authority than intelligence, she asserts, because "it is a rule-breaker" (p. 86). In her meditation on beauty, Hampl attempts to define the power of that authority first by dividing the subject into its constituent parts: the striving for personal beauty, the physical beauty of the natural world or the "made" beauty of art, and the cultivation of an aesthetic sensibility— one that judges and values things by their beauty. After separating the parts, Hampl admits they become hopelessly entangled with one another. "The word, unfortunately, is a touchstone for too many things: beauty has become a switchboard through which I route and connect the various desires and disappointments of my own life and also what I sense more confusedly are those of the culture" (p. 114).

"If we use the same word for vastly different subjects, I believe in their relation before I can prove it" (p. 114). Hampl ultimately concludes that for Americans "beauty rests in our perception of our geographical body . . . we know that the land used to be beautiful . . . and then we came. We have not been able to use our past, more specifically our folk heritage, as other cultures have" since "the folk have often not been an indigenous peasantry, but an oppressed minority" (p. 121). Hampl reasons that this creates a yearning in Americans to recover a past, to dig up their roots, a gesture against "our impoverished sense of beauty, our grudge against loveliness" (p. 126). These are the reasons that propel Hampl back to Prague, the "golden Pralia" that brought tears to her grandmother's eyes at the onset of *A Romantic Education*.

The third section of *A Romantic Education* chronicles that trip, lavishing attention on the light and shadow of another "river city," feeling kinship with not only the city of her grandparents, but Kafka's city, Rilke's birthplace, Mozart's city. But as her trip continues, as she absorbs the ruined quality of a city "on its knees," she "recognized the truth of beauty: that it is brokenness" (p. 151). She ceases to be a "reverse immigrant"—"I sought no one, no sign of my family or any ethnic heritage that might be mine. I was, simply, in the most beautiful place I had ever seen, and it was grimy and sad and broken" (p. 151). Relieved of some of the weight of her quest, Hampl goes to museums, visits some friends. Two years later she returns to Prague, and this visit is characterized by dialogues with several friends who argue with her about European history, the effect of western culture on "middle Europe," the relation of poetry to a cultural past, the "value" of the Vietnam War. Her visit ends on an elegiac tone, with vows to return, and also with the conviction that what resonates in the memory can be retrieved at will.

Like Sarton's metaphor of "Renaissance portraiture" defining a self against its appropriate background, or Hellman's metaphor of the old paint that shows through a new configuration in "Pentimento," Hampl also chooses a metaphoric vehicle to describe the autobiographical process: alchemy. Prague was the "alchemical capital" of Europe until the defeat of the Czech nation, she tells us. She laments its loss, since alchemy was "one of the places" where science and religion were fused. The gold of the alchemists was "spiritual and transformative," a token of exchange that united intellectual inquiry and spiritual enlargement. Hampl sees this holistic exchange as the function of autobiographical metaphor—taking the unalloyed metals of the past and transforming them through "the golden light of metaphor" into narratives that stimulate the mind and enlarge the heart.

Memory then is Sarton's "background," Hellman's "ellipsis," and Hampl's "pig iron"—essentially a horizontal continuum punctuated by events, disputes, controversies of time and place. "The golden light of metaphor" creates Sarton's "essence," Hellman's "silhouette," Hampl's "alchemy" illuminating the dark, undifferentiated streets. Metaphor functions as a vertical axis plunging into time, uncovering or constructing meaning and emotional significance.

One danger lies in sentimentalizing the past, a trap that snaps shut on Eudora Welty's much publicized and much praised chronicle of her childhood, *One Writer's Beginnings* (1984). As Carolyn Heilbrun remarks in *Writing a Woman's Life* (1989): "No memoir has been more admired and loved in recent years than Eudora Welty's *One Writer's Beginnings*. Yet I think there exists a real danger for women in books like Welty's in the nostalgia and romanticizing in which the author, and we in reading them, indulge" (p. 13). Heilbrun objects to the myth of the supportive family happily nourishing the talent of the young writer evident in *One Writer's Beginnings*. She finds it a "camouflage" for the painful and hard-won values apparent in Welty's fiction. Her stories and novels "rescue her from nostalgia," Heilbrun writes, yet *One Writer's Beginnings* pictures a young Welty's "docile acceptance of what is given . . . a simpler world, with simpler values broadly accepted" (p. 13). Nostalgia, Heilbrun believes, is especially dangerous for women since it is often a "mask for unrecognized anger," an avoidance of critiquing one's culture. As Patricia Spacks observes in her essay "Selves in Hiding" (1980), women writing about their own lives "fail directly to emphasize their own importance, though writing in a genre which implies self-assertion and self-display" (p. 14). Spacks notes: "Although each author has significant, sometimes dazzling accomplishments

to her credit, each shrinks from claiming that they either sought the responsibilities they ultimately bore or were in any way ambitious" (p. 23).

Welty seems in *One Writer's Beginnings* to wish to poise herself between
the insignificant and the significant, to locate the extraordinary *within* the
ordinary experience. "I am a writer who came of a sheltered life" she says
of growing up in Jackson, Mississippi, where she still lives at 85, in her
parents' house. "A sheltered life can be a daring life as well. For all serious
daring starts from within." Her account of how she moved slowly toward
her vocation as a writer is divided into three sections: "Listening," "Learning
to See," and "Finding a Voice." In each, how the writer locates a voice is
central, and Welty's distinctive voice is audible in all the descriptions (perhaps all the more evident because these were designed first as lectures to
be delivered in the spring of 1988). The voice is quiet, deliberate, and droll,
and descriptions rove lovingly over details of vanished small town southern
life: the acquisition of the first family automobile, storytelling on the ve-
randah, Sunday afternoon rides in the country. In recording these details
Welty casts herself as one "on whom nothing was lost." She seems also to
have enjoyed family love and security to a degree rare among twentieth-
century writers.

Her father, an insurance man who grew up in Ohio, and her mother,
a schoolteacher from the West Virginia mountains, dominate the second
section of the book—particularly since they are illustrated by a series of
striking photographs (Welty is an accomplished photographer) and detailed
in summer car trips to both sets of Welty's grandparents. These two journeys Welty suggests shaped her early notions of the short story.

> with the passage of time I could look back on them and see them bringing
> me news, discoveries, premonitions, promises—I still can; they still do. When
> I did begin to write, the short story was a shape that had already formed
> itself and stood waiting in the back of my mind. (p. 49)

What she writes about in her fiction she surely also intends to apply
to *One Writer's Beginnings*, in which these comments appear:

> Writing . . . is one way of discovering *sequence*, of stumbling upon cause
> and effect in the happenings of a writer's own life. This has been the case
> with me. Connections slowly emerge. Like distant landmarks you are ap-
> proaching, cause and effect begin to align themselves, draw closer together.
> Experiences too indefinite of outline in themselves to be recognized for them-
> selves connect and are identified as a larger shape. And suddenly light is
> thrown back, as when your train makes a curve, showing there has been a
> mountain of meaning rising behind you on the way you've come, is rising
> there still, proven now through retrospect. (p. 98)

At one point Welty tells the reader that "as an adolescent I was a slammer of drawers and a packer of suitcases. I was responsible for scenes." But she continues:

> of all my strong emotions, anger is the one least responsible for any of my work. I don't write out of anger. For one thing, simply as a fiction writer, I am minus an adversary—except, of course, that of time—and for another thing, the act of writing in itself brings me happiness.

Certainly it is not my task to dispute Welty's contention that the act of writing results in delight, nor do I think Carolyn Heilbrun would challenge the long revered observation that Welty "loves all of her characters," even those caught at moments of limitation, racial prejudice, and social injustice. What does seem disputable is that Welty writes "minus an adversary," since the effect of a Welty story like "Where Is the Voice Coming From?" (where she climbs into the consciousness of the murderer of Medgar Evers, the civil rights activist who was shot in Jackson, Mississippi in front of his home) is shock and revolt. Surely the intention of that shock and revolt is to illumine the *why* of such an act and, in understanding, prevent it from happening again.

Similarly, Phoenix Jackson, the aged Grandma of Welty's often-anthologized "A Worn Path," for all her dignity and sense of self-worth, and even embarked as she is on her mission of love, is a terrifying example of what went wrong in the South and how acceptance of its consequences is never enough. Welty's fiction, loving as it is and tolerant of its characters as it may be, is also conscious of Mississippi as the poorest state in the union, and of the southern past as one of slavery, secession, defeat, reconstruction, and decline. Welty records rather than judges, but she records *in such a way* that the task of assessment falls to the reader. Welty assumes in her fiction a *collaborative* reader, one who will advocate for some of her issues. Where is that "pact" in her autobiography? Where is her "real subject"?

Sally Wolff, in an interview with Eudora Welty (*The Southern Review*, Winter 1990), tried to lead the reticent author to make connections between *One Writer's Beginnings* and her highly autobiographical novel, *The Optimist's Daughter*.

> WOLFF: One of the issues raised at the recent conference on southern autobiography is whether there is a distinct body of work that might be thought of as southern autobiography. Do you think certain aspects of southern life and culture might predispose writers to autobiography?
>
> WELTY: Yes, I think probably so, don't you? It occurs to me that southerners take certain things for granted—such as certain classes, certain

strictures, different backgrounds—people immediately make certain assumptions. Southerners want to place everybody. This was especially true in former times, when someone might say "Oh, so-and-so, his father was so-and-so." It used to be so simple—you might be born on the wrong side of the track. I remember as a child being taught not to make this count. I was warned against it. But it's a way southerners have of locating themselves.

WOLFF: What else in southerners might encourage them to write about themselves?

WELTY: It's entertaining when it's done well. It helps you get a narrative sense of continuity when there are so many stories through the generations—something that connects people together. I missed that when I lived in other parts of the country. People were friends but had no sense of their ancestors. No one was interested. I did have a good friend—David Daiches—who invited me to visit his family in Edinburgh. The family I met there was so warm and welcoming. His three aunts met me at the door with arms extended. I felt at home with them. In the South we combine a feeling of family and of place. They are twin strands, the sense of family and place. I didn't grow up with this sense of the whole family. As you know from *One Writer's Beginnings*, much of the family was away.

WOLFF: In West Virginia?

WELTY: Yes.

WOLFF: The feeling of being somewhat isolated from extended family also comes through in *The Optimist's Daughter* in Becky and Laurel's memories about West Virginia.

WELTY: Yes, I used it in the work in general. I used the point of view of the child coming to something new. I did the same thing in *Delta Wedding* where the child's perspective is a narrative device to lead the reader into something new. In lots of stories it's the stranger to the family that provides this perspective. Maybe that is my point of view.

Welty proves elusive, even to this veteran interviewer, as she circles the questions and retools them to her own purpose.

WOLFF: I'm interested in the remark you made earlier that when you were writing *Optimist's Daughter* you did not envision yourself in the novel. Laurel has characteristics which are both similar to and unlike yours, doesn't she?

WELTY: Yes. In a wider sense, I would say it was my own inquiring mind that corresponds to the girl's in the novel, to the effort to understand your roots and the decision in the end that you can't be held back by the past. I used things that would be useful in the novel. The war was very important, for instance. My friend in World War II married into—well, when someone was lost—like Phil is—I knew what that feeling was like. How could I not have? That was a war people believed in. We still had the belief in World War II that war could be ended by licking the Nazis. The difference in attitude toward war now is striking. Some of my friends put on a production at the New Stage of the songs of Irving Berlin. The young girls were giggling at songs like "Over There!" and the director stopped them and said, "When those songs were written, they meant that." It was a bad war. The boys we knew were involved and we were with them. These young people in the theater couldn't conceive of fighting for a cause. This applies to Phil. The part in the novel about the kamikaze happened to my brother Walter. He was in the Navy at Okinawa, and later he was asked, "How close have you come to a kamikaze?" and he said, "Close enough to shake hands with." So I put that in the story. Who could ever make up a thing like that?

WOLFF: No one could. Was Phil made up?

WELTY: Phil is an amalgamation of a lot of boys I knew. My older brother, the middle child, has some of his characteristics—those double-jointed thumbs, and he was an architect. Phil has not got his character, though. Although he did make a breadboard. But no one ever acted badly about it.

WOLFF: No one ever acted the way Fay does?

WELTY: Not in my family: but I've seen a-many, a-many. And anyone who's ever had anyone in the hospital will recognize the people who sit in the waiting rooms and eat and drink and talk. I wouldn't want anyone to think that I was using their sick in the novel, but these things come back to me, like air, and I use them.

However self-deprecating, modest, and unassuming a tone Welty's autobiography employs, her stories "know better." How the disenfranchised find ways to tell their own stories, to exert their own authority *is* a Welty plot. How the voiceless gain a voice *is* Welty dialogue. And how the vulnerable character asserts a claim to life *is* a Welty protagonist. Despite the sugar-coated rhetoric of *One Writer's Beginnings*, her fiction displays a sensibility that continues to "slam drawers," to "pack suitcases," and to "make scenes." Quiet in tone, Welty's stories are combustible in effect; they move a reader to unease and self-assessment. The "daring," the risk that so permeates the stories, is nowhere apparent in *One Writer's Beginnings*, unless one feels its presence by its *insistent absence*. To borrow Patricia Hampl's terminology, Eudora Welty seems to return to her childhood more as a "tourist," camera in hand, than as a "pilgrim," searching for meaning.

Silencing: Repression and Self-Censorship

The difficulties of arriving at one's real subject and plumbing that subject as a "pilgrim" are particularly complicated for the female autobiographer. "Telling the truth" and "telling it slant" are parallel injunctions that elicit a shock of recognition in most female readers. The long history of encoding "messages," the anxiety of transmission, the shifting ground on which self-knowledge stands are all multiply conflictual in the female autobiographer.

Forces that threaten, censor, or attempt to shape the female autobiographical expression are examined in three widely read texts published in the late 1970s. Tillie Olsen's *Silences* (1978), Adrienne Rich's *On Lies, Secrets and Silence* (1979), and Sandra Gilbert and Susan Gubar's *The Madwoman in the Attic* (1979) explore societal repression and self-censorship as forces that bury the real subjects in women's writing and that complicate the task of truth-telling.

Gilbert and Gubar locate censoring in what they call the "anxiety of authorship," the fear arising from the recognition that authorship confers authority and that authority seems "to the female artist to be by definition inappropriate to her sex" (p. 51). Accustomed to being neutered or assigned to "attic space," the female artist struggles to identify her own voice, locate and utilize effectively her own materials.

Rather than stressing the absence of a stake in the world of letters for women, Tillie Olsen emphasizes the disproportionately heavy stake women occupy in the labor force; their "world of labor" (Olsen concentrates frequently on low-income women, often single mothers) prevents them from full literary participation. In *Silences*, she traces their sense of discouragement back to the differing "climate of expectation" generated for male children versus female children. What do we teach our female children to expect of life? How can female writers trust the validity of their own experience when "having a career" forecloses on "fulfillment as a woman"? The results, says Olsen, are successive generations of silenced, or apologetic, women locked in a process she defines as the "unnatural thwarting of what struggles to come into being but cannot" (p. xi).

But it is Adrienne Rich who hones the keen edge on the definition of silencing. In *On Lies, Secrets and Silence*, she explores female writers who, like the Aunt Jennifer of her famous poem, "Aunt Jennifer's Tigers," were "ringed with the ordeals [they were] mastered by." Using her own experience as the mother of three sons, wife of a Harvard economics professor, and a poet struggling to find a voice of her own (not the Audenesque imitation that had already won her the Yale Younger Series Award), she determines that "traditional roles" nullify the crucial conditions needed for a writer's success.

A certain freedom of mind is needed—freedom to press on, to enter the currents of your thought like a glider pilot, knowing that your motion can be sustained, that the buoyancy of your attention will not be suddenly snatched away. Moreover, if the imagination is to transcend and transform experience it has to question, to challenge, to conceive of alternatives, perhaps to the very life you are living at that moment. You have to be free to

play around with the notion that day might be night, love might be hate;
nothing can be too sacred for the imagination to turn into its opposite or to
call experimentally by another name . . . to be a female human being trying
to fulfill traditional female functions in a traditional way is in direct conflict
with the subversive function of the imagination . . . there must be ways, and
we will be finding out more and more about them, in which the energy of
creation and the energy of relation can be united. But in those years I always felt the conflict as a failure of love in myself. (pp. 43–44)

The need to float on currents of thought "like a glider pilot," the need
to exercise the "subversive imagination" and yet the equally strongly felt
need to successfully perform "traditional female tasks in traditional ways,"
focus the recurrent crises reflected in the journals and letters of Sylvia Plath
and Anne Sexton. In *On Lies, Secrets and Silence*, Rich uses the occasion of a
memorial service following Sexton's 1974 suicide to demonstrate the
murderous consequences of believing "the images patriarchy has held up
to us" (p. 123).

Among those lies she lists "self-trivialization . . . believing the lie that
women are not capable of major creations." Another is "horizontal hostility"—contempt for other women, a kind of "self hatred." Another is "ad-
diction"—to romantic love mythology, to sex, to drugs, to male approval,
to anything that offers a "blanket of blankness" (p. 122). In angrily decry-
ing Sexton's suicide, Rich asks all women to grow "better poised for the
act of survival" (p. 123). The autobiographical writings of Anne Sexton
and Sylvia Plath as well as biographers' modeling of their lives offer dramatic proof of the difficulties inherent in constructing a self better "poised
for survival." Not only are the authors themselves conflicted about what
is "true" about their own life experience, but their biographers fail to credit
metaphor with representational rather than factual content or discuss
memory as sufficiently different from chronology. By failing to understand
that autobiography constructs an imaginary order, one the reader resignifies by first accepting the construct, then "correcting" it by returning, in
Lacanian terms, from the realm of the Imaginary to the Real, Sexton's and
Plath's lives become fodder for biographers' distortions and manipulations.
The autobiographical "I" can only "stand in" for the ever-elusive subject.

Anne Sexton: A Self-Portrait in Letters (1977) catches the urgency of the
moment, the mind in the act of expressing itself—qualities evident in much
of Anne Sexton's poetry. Her head-on intimacy was a source of real dis-
comfort, however, early in her poetic career. Her teacher, John Holmes,
wrote her an admonitory letter after seeing the manuscript that was eventually to become *To Bedlam and Part Way Back*, advising her not to publish
the poems she had written about her mental breakdowns.

> I am uneasy . . . that what looks like a brilliant beginning might turn out to be so self-centered and so narrowed a diary that it would be clinical only. Something about asserting the hospital and psychiatric experiences seems to me very selfish—all a forcing others to listen to you, and nothing given the listeners, nothing that teaches them or helps them. . . . It bothers me that you use poetry this way. It's all a release for you but what is it for anybody else except a spectacle of someone experiencing release?[2]

Sexton tells Holmes that his rejection of her poetry is defensive, for art tells not a private but a collective truth, one that "includes and reveals him." (Holmes's first wife was a suicide, and he himself a recovering alcoholic.)

To see that "collective truth," even when its terms were horrible, was Anne Sexton's literary calling. The truths that "include" and "reveal" are everywhere apparent in her letters. Many of them are to fellow writers and supporters or informed critics of her work: W.D. Snodgrass, Maxine Kumin, Tillie Olsen, Robert Lowell, Frederick Morgan.

From these letters it is clear she places the issue of human intimacy at the center of her writing: It is the source of poetic language. To a psychiatrist friend, Sexton wrote:

> It is hard to define. When I was first sick I was thrilled . . . to get into the Nut House. At first, of course, I was just scared and crying and very quiet (who me!) but then I found this girl (very crazy of course) (like me I guess) who talked language. What a relief! I mean, well . . . someone! And then later, a while later, and quite a while, I found out that [Dr.] Martin talked language. (p. 244)

When she began to write poetry and attend workshops, she discovered another group who spoke "language." As Diane Middlebrook, Sexton's biographer, argues, and Alicia Ostriker corroborates, what Sexton means by language is something "compressed, elliptical, metaphoric. Schizophrenics use language this way, and so do poets: figurative language is the term Sexton might have used here to indicate that the crucible of formation was urgent need" (Ostriker, p. 8). Letter after letter reveals her belief that a writer must acknowledge the pain of personal experience rather than attempting to "avoid knowing what is happening."

> Everyone has somewhere the ability to mask the events of pain and sorrow, call it shock . . . when someone dies for instance you have this shock that carries you over it, makes it bearable. But the creative person must not use this mechanism any more than they have to in order to keep breathing. (*Letters*, p. 306)

Writing is *real* because it is the one thing that will save (and I do mean save) another life. [Emphasis added.]

J. Holmes wasn't impressed with "Heart's Needle" . . . and now I have figured out why. He is afraid of something that real. People are afraid of people, especially poets. As I said to Fred Morgan, in discussing how I came to know you and how I first came to be influenced by you . . . I read "Heart's Needle" and I changed. It made me see myself new. In seeing you, in feeling your marvellous [sic] restrained sense of immediate loss, I saw my own loss in a new color. And I changed. . . . I don't mean to imply that I have written anything as good. I have not. . . . Tho' Rose Morgan said to me, about "The Double Image," "thank you, Anne, for writing that poem" . . . and Fred said, in talking of the final insight of the poem . . .

> I who was never quite sure
> about being a girl, need another
> life, another image to remind me.
> And this was my worst guilt; you could not cure
> nor soothe it. I made you to find me.

—he looked kind of funny and said, something about those lines really got to him. And how he guessed he understood better and better why his first wife kept wanting and having more and more children. "She made them to find herself, but couldn't." . . . What I'm trying to say is that, I think a poem that can do that to people, make them see themselves through yourself, is valid . . . not too personal. (p. 58, emphasis added)

As she saw it, poetry was the opposite of self-protection, a mirror or reflexive medium in which the reader sees "self." Otherwise, it peters out in self-regarding madness, "snail-like, curled up inside itself."

To follow Sexton's letters chronologically is to feel how valiantly she struggled to keep poetry functioning as a therapeutic medium—not simply for herself but for others who might, in the face of something *real*, be changed. Sadly the letters also reflect declining stability, waning energy, and sporadic outbreaks of genuine mental illness. Most are reflections of her "two selves": "good Anne" and "bad Anne." Although she seems to believe the voice of good Anne dominates the letters, another bleaker voice authors the poems, and yet another "bad" voice is responsible for the rages, the paranoia, the manipulation, and the alcoholism periodically evident in her life. In fact the letters reveal all of those selves, the final 200 or so chronicling impossible demands of old friends, a divorce from her husband, incredible generosity to a few burgeoning writers, and concerns for the safety and well-being of her daughters.

Sexton willed this book into existence, appointing her older daughter as literary executor, carefully saving carbon copies of all her letters. Accordingly, her daughter and Lois Ames, coeditors of the volumes, resisted the impulse to cosmetically alter the "self-portrait," and we see Sexton, as Margaret Atwood (1977) wrote in a review of the volume, as "neither heroine nor victim, but as an angular, complex, often loving and at times rather insufferable human being" (p. 15). The letters close to the end of her life reveal how crafty she was in distorting situations not working to her best advantage. And although she was making a substantial income in royalties, teaching fees, and readings, she became obsessed with money and real and imagined debts. She repeatedly told friends she was responsible for her children's education and support, which were, in truth, paid for by others. Her drinking escalated sharply and her death was "not unexpected" (*Letters*, p. 378).

Her final letter in the volume suggests she was acutely aware of how her death would affect others—especially her children. In a letter written in April 1969 (she committed suicide in October 1974) to her daughter Linda, she tries to comfort and hold, anticipating that time when physical contact would be impossible. "Be your own woman. Belong to those you love. Talk to my poems, and talk to your heart. I'm in both if you need me" (p. 380).

Maxine Kumin, best friend and confidante, provides this summary, in "How It Was" (1988), of Anne's effect on others, everywhere apparent in the letters.

> It is true that she attracted the worshipful attention of a cult group pruriently interested in her suicidal impulses, her psychotic breakdowns, her frequent hospitalizations. It must equally be acknowledged that her very frankness succored many who clung to her poems as to the Holy Grail. (p. 210)

Several of the crucial letters as well as co-editing chores in *Anne Sexton: A Self-Portrait in Letters* fell to Lois Ames, close friend of Sexton who was also working on a biography of Sylvia Plath. Her acquaintance with Plath, she writes in "Notes Toward a Biography" (1970), was at first one of circumstances, since they "attended the same high school, church and college, went to the same parties and dances" (p. 155). Two years after Plath's death, and with Ted Hughes's "generous permission," Lois Ames went to England to talk with people who had known Plath at various times in her life. She found most of them open and cooperative, although she discovered "a marked contrast between recollection of her at different ages" (p. 155). "A marked contrast" seems ironically understated in light of the furious disputes that swirled about the publication in 1975 of Plath's letters to her mother, *Letters Home: Correspondence 1950–1963*; her journals, published with a foreword by Ted Hughes in 1982; her "unsanctioned" biography, *Sylvia Plath: A Biography*, written by Linda Wagner-Martin in

1987 (in which the Hughes family refused permission to quote from Plath's work unless substantial cuts were made); and Anne Stevenson's "sanctioned" biography, *Bitter Fame: A Life of Sylvia Plath*, appearing in 1989. Plath's autobiographical experience presents a kind of minefield for stalking biographers, since not only was she capable of engendering widely different responses in others, but she also vacillated in her self-assessments, often swinging through violent mood shifts within any given week. And like Lillian Hellman, she was prone to doctoring the truth—skewering it to please her hard-working, self-effacing mother in many of her "letters home" as if to justify the self-sacrifice that sent her to Smith and Cambridge, or less benignly shaping the event, as she does in some journal entries so as to cast herself as the leading actress in the drama of the moment.

Not surprisingly, Plath's suicide at the age of 30 at the height of her poetic reputation, followed by the publication of the *Ariel* poems—many of them self-lacerating and intense, some healthy, some prurient—unleashed a tidal wave of interest about her life. Like Sexton, Plath wrote naked poems about suicide, hatred of the father, the ambivalence of motherhood; so readers who were magnetically drawn to the poems also felt an eerie intimacy with her life experience.

Anne Sexton and Sylvia Plath were friends, sharing membership in a Boston University Poetry Workshop directed by Robert Lowell, repairing afterward to the lounge-bar of the Ritz to eat free potato chips and drink martinis. They were drawn to one another both as poets and as failed suicides, and it is Sexton, in "The Barfly Ought to Sing," who gives us one perceptive window on this period in Plath's life.

> In the lounge-bar of the Ritz, not a typical bar at all, but very plush, deep dark red carpeting, red leather chairs around polite little tables and with waiters, white coated and awfully hushed where one knew upon stepping down the firm velvet red steps that he was entering *something*, we entered. The waiters knew their job. They waited on the best of Boston, or at least, celebrities. We always hoped they'd make a mistake in our case and think us some strange Hollywood types. There had to be something to explain all our books, our snowboots, our clutter of poems, our address, our quick and fiery conversation. . . .
>
> Often, very often, Sylvia and I would talk at length about our first suicides; at length, in detail and in depth between the free potato chips. Suicide is, after all, the opposite of the poem. Sylvia and I often talked opposites. We talked death with burned-up intensity, both of us drawn to it like moths to an electric light bulb. . . . We talked death and this was life for us. . . . I think we were . . . stimulated by it . . . as if death made us a little more real at the moment. (p. 175)

If as Ted Hughes, the husband from whom she was estranged at the time of her death, contends in the Introduction to her *Journals*, "she had none of the usual guards and remote controls to protect herself from her own reality" (p. 20), it is natural that many in the general reading public hovered over her life experience for clues to the intensity, to the vivacity, and to the death wish evident in her poems. Was Otto Plath, the German-born scientist father encoded as a Nazi in the infamous "Daddy," really to blame for inscribing female passivity on his daughter and then dying before its terms could be renegotiated in adulthood? Was Aurelia Plath to blame for living an all-too-vicarious life through her talented daughter, forcing Sylvia into an endless cycle of striving and achievement? Did Ted Hughes, in refusing to release some primary materials and destroying the journals chronicling the last two years of their life together—years that included his infidelity and her jealous rage—attempt to sidestep his own guilt under the camouflage of "protecting the children"? Surely these were some of the questions intriguing readers who waited eagerly for the next installment of Plath materials or who bought *Letters Home* and *Journals* with the expectation of a crime solver.

Interestingly, *Letters* and *Journals* (at least the ones readers are permitted to see) reveal a masked Sylvia, one who adjusted her tone and her content to the expectations of a reader. If in her poems she works without a safety net, her letters reveal all sorts of safety nets. And if, as Alicia Ostriker suggests in *Writing Like a Woman*, Plath's strategy in her poems consisted of "having learned to see the skull beneath the skin, she threw away the skin" (p. 47), the journals and letters are all skin, connective tissue guarding against the dark hollows of recognizable skull. This makes them fascinating as auto-biographical narratives, for in them we detect the ways Plath wants to be seen, the achievements she wishes were easily hers, the risks she dare not take, the fears she cannot acknowledge or entirely leave behind. Plath's letters and journals, even as expurgated by Hughes and cosmetically touched up by Aurelia Plath's selection process, provide a lesson in how others can manipulate autobiographical materials to create a "self-portrait" as well as how the subject herself decides on the terms of her own self-inscription.

What shapes Plath's own "self-portrait" are two recurrent drives that together constitute her real subject: an immense will to succeed and a baffling search for a self that will propel a successful career in poetry and also sustain a happy and productive marriage. Letters and journal entries, particularly during her college years at Smith, link an idealized domesticity with female dependence.

> I dislike being a girl, because as such I must come to realize I cannot be
> a man. In other words, I must pour my energies through the direction and

force of my mate. My only free act is choosing or refusing that mate. (*Journals*, p. 6)

> I wonder if art divorced from normal and conventional living is as vital as art combined with living: in a word, would marriage sap my creative energy and annihilate my desire for written and pictorial expression . . . or would I [if I married] achieve a fuller expression in art as well as in the creation of children? (p. 7)

By the age of 20 she's saying:

> I need a strong mate: I do not want to accidentally crush and subdue him like a steamroller. . . . I must find a strong potential powerful mate who can counter my vibrant dynamic self: sexual and intellectual. (p. 38)

> Let's face it, I am in danger of wanting my personal absolute to be a demigod of a man. . . . I want a romantic nonexistent hero. (p. 47)

After she meets Hughes in Cambridge, *only two weeks later*, he has become the "demigod."

> Please let him come; let me have him for this British spring. Please, please. . . . Oh, he is here; my black marauder. (p. 116)

The myth of the fierce and equally talented romantic hero who will father her into her fullest self in life and art is doomed and is also her own clear creation. Plath is striking a devastating bargain, even as she sophomorically casts herself in the role of "loving that black marauder."

After she is married, a "perfect union" that she presents as a "gift" to her mother, she exudes the celebratory wish-fulfillment prose that frequently characterizes her *Letters Home*.

> We will publish a bookshelf of books between us before we perish! And a batch of brilliant healthy children. . . . I am so glad Ted is first . . . it is as if he is the perfect male counterpart to my own self. (p. 153)

A year later she lists in her journal all the female poets toward whom she felt both admiring and rivalrous. Three are living: May Swenson, Isabella Gardner, "and most close Adrienne Cecile Rich." Three years older than Plath, Rich met her at Radcliffe that spring and is characterized by her as: "little, round and stumpy, all vibrant short black hair, great sparkling black eyes and a tulip red umbrella: honest, frank, forthright and even opinionated" (p. 167).

Plath scrutinizes particularly those whose sexual choices were different from hers, Elizabeth Bishop and Marianne Moore: "My old admiration for the strong, if lesbian, woman. The relief of limitation as a price for balance and surety" (p. 179). Yet she fears being barren and rhapsodizes about pregnancy.

> I would bear children until my change of life if that were possible. I want a home of our children, little animals, flowers, vegetables, fruits. I want to be an Earth-Mother in the deepest, richest sense. (p. 311)

Actual pregnancy brings a cooler head, but this sort of insight seems only temporary (or carefully muted in other letters or journal entries).

> Children might humanize me. But I must rely on them for nothing. Fable of children changing existence and character as absurd as fable of marriage doing it. Here I am, the same old sourdough. (p. 371)

Plath's own characterizations, taken on the run, reveal the attraction of the myths of "mother" and "wife" central to her time. At the same time they inscribe an artistic myth, one carefully adjusted to the "reader" who—years ahead—will sift through the journals for clues to the poetry, or one adjusted to her mother's eyes, that long-suffering patient woman who unwittingly (and certainly unconsciously) placed on her daughter the heavy responsibility of keeping them both happy.

There are, however, other chiselers, who censor and delete her self-inscriptions. One cannot, for example, use the *Journals* as a gloss to Sylvia Plath's poetry—even with all her hedging, distortion, and filtering—as they do not cover the period 1959–1963, when her major work was written. Ted Hughes describes the selection process as one of "curtailing"; Aurelia Plath simply says she selected letters that present her daughter's "account of herself."

In the Foreword to Hughes's edition of the *Journals*, he says:

> Two more notebooks survived for a while, maroon-backed ledgers like the 57–59 volume, and continued the record from late '59 to within three days of her death. The last of these contained entries for several months, and I destroyed it because I did not want her children to have read it (in those days I regarded forgetfulness as an essential part of survival). The other disappeared. (p. xv)

The period covered by destroyed or "disappearing" journals includes Plath and Hughes's return to England; the birth of a daughter in 1960; the publication of *The Colossus*, Plath's first book of poetry; a miscarriage and emergency appendectomy; a contract with *The New Yorker*; the writing and publication of *The Bell Jar*; the birth of a son in 1962; an affair by Hughes that led to their separation in October 1962; Plath taking the children, aged 2½ and 9 months, to London in a desperately cold winter; the writing of 25 poems in November and 12 more before her death on February 11, 1963. Small wonder that Hughes admits ruefully: "Those years produced the work that made her name." One hundred thirty manuscript pages of a novel called *Double Exposure* were also lost.

Not surprisingly, this broken record of crucial life experiences has produced biographies widely off the mark, inaccurate in many respects, and frequently brandishing more than one "axe to grind." Two of the most recent examples serve to illustrate the impact literary executorship—its cooperativeness or its hostility—has on the final portrait to emerge, even when using "autobiographical data." Linda Wagner-Martin, in her biography of Plath, records this frustrating exchange with Olwyn Hughes, Ted's sister, now the literary executor of the Sylvia Plath estate.

> Most of Plath's manuscripts are housed at either Lilly Library at Indiana University, Bloomington, or the Rare Book Room at Smith College. At the estate's mandate, one group of Plath's papers at Smith has been sealed until the year 2013; another is closed until after the deaths of both her mother and her younger brother. Publication of the Plath materials in those libraries is controlled by Ted Hughes. . . .
>
> When I began researching this biography, I contacted Olwyn Hughes. . . . [Olwyn] was initially cooperative. As she read later chapters . . . her cooperation diminished substantially. Olwyn wrote me at great length, usually in argument with my views about the life and development of Plath. Ted Hughes responded to a reading of the manuscript in draft form with suggestions for changes that filled fifteen pages and would have meant a deletion of more than 15,000 words . . . requests for changes continued and I concluded that permissions [to quote from Plath's work] would be granted only if I agreed to change the manuscript to reflect the Hugheses' points of view. (p. 14)

It is not surprising then to discover that the version of Plath's life Wagner-Martin tells is heavily weighted toward Sylvia's American roots, her early literary mentors, her relationship with her parents and brother, her Smith years, and her year in Cambridge, all amply documented by "more than two hundred people who agreed to be interviewed."

The Wagner-Martin biography tends to see Plath's final two years as ones of acute personal struggle, fierce competition as her career surged ahead of her husband's, and bitter rejection after his affair shortly following the birth of their son, Nicholas. For Wagner-Martin, Plath is intensely alone in those last months, far from her family and friends and "divorced" from the orbit of Ted's. "In death as in life, Sylvia Plath is something of an American in exile" (p. 247).

Two years later Anne Stevenson, a poet and reviewer who has spent most of her adult life in England, published her version of the Plath story. "*Bitter Fame* seeks to put right a perverse legend . . . her family and friends have been helpless to dispel the posthumous miasma of fantasy, rumor, politics, and ghoulish gossip," the cover blurb announces. Stevenson accords her greatest debt to Olwyn Hughes. In the first page of her text, this "Author's Note" appears:

> In writing this biography, I have received a great deal of help from Olwyn Hughes, literary agent to the Estate of Sylvia Plath. Ms. Hughes's contributions to the text have made it almost a work of dual authorship. (p. x)

Accordingly, the view she presents of Plath is one of an intense, volatile character who had always borne within her the seeds of her own destruction. Ted Hughes appears almost saintly in his constant care, literary guidance, and overwhelming patience with her jealous rages: "He cared too much." His suppression and/or destruction of her journals is accounted "understandable" in light of his own need for "the privacy of his life and the lives of his children" (p. xii), and since his friends who knew them in those last years were "reluctant to make their memories public until the children grew up," she includes memoirs from three of Ted's friends who spent time with Hughes and Plath in the final two years of her life: Lucas Myers, Dido Merwin, and Richard Murphy. She does not interview either Mrs. Plath or Warren Plath. Perhaps the most spectacular inclusion in this volume is Dido Merwin's diatribe against Plath, appropriately titled "Vessel of Wrath: A Memoir of Sylvia Plath," in which Merwin excuses Hughes's infidelity on the grounds that Plath's jealousy provoked it, and characterizes Plath in passages like these: "She was like a car with no reverse gear and increasingly faulty brakes, a disastrous combination that was the nexus of her obsessive self-regard, her lack of conscience, her unwisdom, and of course, her jealousy problem" (p. 322). Dido Merwin ends by verifying the truth of her memoir since it was composed in the shadow of death. Hers cannot be considered "malicious retaliation," she says, since she has been "diagnosed as having cancer with a poor prognosis." Such a condition, she says, quoting Dr. Johnson, "concentrates the mind wonderfully" (p. 347).[3]

I contend that there is "truth value" to be found in the letters and journals of Sexton and Plath, but it is far from harvested "objective fact" or the personal agendas of eye witnesses. Instead, both poets employ images, metaphors, extended analogies to encode and reveal their deepest fears and ambitions (e.g., the "language of crazies," the "snail curled up inside itself," the myth of the "black marauder," the "same old sourdough"). To treat their self-inscriptions without accounting for these images is rather like offering an interpretation of *Citizen Kane* without mentioning "Rosebud," or ignoring Bergman's haunting close-up of the Warsaw ghetto child in *Persona*. Each of those images signifies something essential to our comprehension of the entire script. Each suggests its truth content. We depend on the revelatory power of what the image signifies. In filmic language such an image is an "imaginary signifier" (Christian Metz), the process that allows the spectator to accept an image as the substitute for reality.[4] In literary language it is the vehicle's (the physical image's) separation from its tenor (associative content to which it is being compared), allowing the reader to grasp one by touching the other. It is this process of image-making, "the inevitable tango of memory and imagination," as Patricia Hampl puts it in "The Need to Say It"—Sarton's essence, Hellman's pentimento, Hampl's alchemy—that causes their scripts to vibrate with meaning.

Notes

1 I am indebted to Lloyd Michaels's discussion of "The Thin Blue Line and the Limits of Documentary" for the distinctions Morris makes between "factual investigation" and stylized and expressionistic filmic renderings of the "truth." In examining the process of documentary film making, Michaels uncovers the "elusive border that separates imagination from truth," an equally elusive zone in autobiography.

2 Diane Wood Middlebrook, "'I Tapped My Own Head': The Apprenticeship of Anne Sexton," in *Coming to Light: American Women Poets in the Twentieth Century*, Middlebrook and Yalom, eds. (Ann Arbor, University of Michigan Press: 1985), pp. 195–203. The censoring efforts of John Holmes are discussed on pp. 202–210.

3 My discussion of biases in biographers' treatments of their subjects was written prior to Janet Malcolm's exhaustive (and exhausting) orchestration of the self-serving motives evident in some of Plath's biographers. See her *The Silent Woman* (*The New Yorker*, August 23 & 30, 1993) for further elucidation of this theme, as well as for her exposé of self—i.e., the journalistic bias within one who investigates biographical bias.

4 I am indebted to Lloyd Michaels for calling this process to my attention. For further analysis see Christian Metz, *The Imaginary Signifier: Psychoanalysis and the Cinema* (Bloomington, Indiana University Press: 1982).

♦ 3 ♦

"The Site of Memory"

Characteristically, the autobiographical act within Anglo-American male literary history has been connected to and defined by a sense of place. The autobiographer/narrator frequently writes as a strategy to defend against or articulate a certain kind of isolation, retreating to a place that vivifies memory. For example, in Thoreau's *Walden*, Emerson's journals, *The Education of Henry Adams*, and Whitman's *Specimen Days*, the personal record intersects history. The window on a life, as recorded by a sensitive and gifted perceiver, also reveals a window on an "age"—one usually characterized by crisis or profound change. The autobiographer becomes a seismograph of the times.

Female autobiographers also place themselves in a context. Their sense of place is much more likely to trigger self-assessments or insights into interior consciousness than to engage the public world's moral or historical issues. Compare *Walden* with Annie Dillard's *Pilgrim at Tinker Creek*, for example. Although both purport to be first-person accounts of "life in the woods," Thoreau is moved to air a variety of worldly grievances: Taxes, a standing army, slavery, and philanthropy are some of his favorite targets. Dillard, by contrast, sees the memoir as "no place from which to launch an attack" but rather positions herself where "time pelted me as if I were standing under a water fountain" in order to become "fully awake." Her subject, she continues in "To Fashion a Text," is the power of the interior life available to her while "time streams in full flood beside [her]" (pp. 58–59).

Without reverting to gender stereotyping (after all, Alfred Kazin, Donald Hall, Willie Morris, Russell Baker, and John Updike—to name a few—write personal memoirs shimmering with a sense of place and an interior consciousness, and Joan Didion, Mary Lee Settle, and Charlayne Hunter-Gault write memoirs with political bite), this chapter explores how female autobiographers use a sense of place to trigger what Toni Morrison calls "emotional memory." It is a term closely allied to Hellman's "pentimento," Sarton's "essences," or Hampl's "alchemy," since it emphasizes how a writer employs selective memory to flood a narrative with meaning.

67

A Sense of Place: The Trigger of "Emotional Memory"

In speaking about the slave narratives that document a portion of her historic past, Morrison, in "The Site of Memory" (1987), laments the lack of interior life they display. Clearly, she understands why recently freed slaves selected the instances they would record with great care: "In shaping the experience to make it palatable to those who were in a position to alleviate it, they were silent about many things, and they 'forgot' many other things" (p. 110). In "lifting the veil" they had dropped on subjects too sensitive to expose, Morrison triggers "emotional memory," a term she aligns with Zora Neale Hurston's "memories within that come out of the material that went to make me"—what Morrison calls the "subsoil of my work" (p. 111)—and yokes it to imagination, which "fills in the blanks" (p. 113).

> So if I'm looking to find and expose a truth about the interior life of people who didn't write it (which doesn't mean that they didn't have it) . . . then the approach that's most productive and most trustworthy for me is the recollection that moves from the image to the text . . . the image comes first and tells me what the "memory" is about. (pp. 113–114)

It is tempting to suggest that as surely as white history veiled black consciousness, so patriarchal history veiled women's self-inscriptions. I'm less interested in parallelisms in censorship here, however, than in the strikingly similar coping mechanisms each minority devised to combat silencing. The route to the "reconstruction of the world" of black consciousness Morrison suggests moves from meaningful image to extrapolated text. Is this not reminiscent of the "single red detail" animating "that world," which Patricia Hampl argues is the way we "live again" in memory? (see Chapter 2). Or is it not closely akin to the process she describes as "memoir writing": "How uncanny to go back in memory to a house from which time has stolen all the furniture, and to find the one remembered chair, and write it so large, so deep, that it furnishes the entire vacant room" ("The Need to Say It," p. 29).

Maxine Kumin is perhaps the writer who comes to mind most immediately when one thinks of memoirists who move from "one chair" to furnishing an "entire room." Were I to ask any group of students of American literature what images pop into the consciousness when thinking of Maxine Kumin's journals, essays, or poems, some of these replies would be virtually guaranteed: horses, mushrooms, jars of preserves, soup kettles, tack rooms, pastures (with fences in ill-repair), abandoned vehicles that stand in meadows like sculptures. The features of a New England landscape, more particularly the topography of the "hardscrabble farm" in New

Hampshire that Kumin shares with her husband Victor, assorted horses, dogs, cats, visiting children and grandchildren, appear and reappear as *leitmotifs* in her work, kernels that—when cracked open—reveal the truths of her life experience.

Similarly, Annie Dillard's explorations of the skin on the back of her mother's hand, or the mosaic of Christ in the apse of Pittsburgh's Shadyside Presbyterian Church, or Kate Simon's Yiddish mother's "talented sewing machine," trigger memories of the "material that went to make me." It is a poet's method of triggering imagination, and, not surprisingly for the female writer, it works to reveal what previously has been concealed. Toni Morrison calls this process "flooding."

> You know, they straightened out the Mississippi River in places, to make room for houses and livable acreage. Occasionally the river floods these places. "Floods" is the word they use, but in fact it is not flooding; it is remembering. Remembering where it used to be. All water has a perfect memory and is forever trying to get back to where it was. Writers are like that: remembering where we were, what valley we ran through, what the banks were like, the light that was there and the route back to our original place. It is emotional memory—what the nerves and the skin remember as well as how it appeared. And a rush of imagination is our "flooding." ("The Site of Memory," p. 119)

Perhaps a good place to start to talk about flooding is in Annie Dillard's Pittsburgh, located at the "golden triangle" where the Allegheny and Monongahela Rivers flow into the Ohio. The setting, Dillard tells us, is organic to her emphasis in *An American Childhood* (1987).

> When everything else has gone from my brain—the President's name, the state capitals, the neighborhoods where I lived, and then my own name and what it was on earth I sought, and then at length the faces of my friends, and finally the faces of my family—when all this has dissolved, what will be left, I believe, is topology: the dreaming memory of land as it lay this way and that. (p. 3)

Land gives shape to consciousness, which converges within the child "as a landing tern touches the outspread feet of its shadow on the sand. . . . Like any child, I slid into myself perfectly fitted, as a diver meets her reflection in a pool" (p. 11). Pittsburgh is the reflection pool Dillard, the diver, enters.

Since this is a book about "waking up," exploring the "vertical motion of consciousness" (p. 11) as caught and shaped by a life in a Pittsburgh suburb in the early 1950s, she "puts in" touchstones of Pittsburgh's topography and historical past.

> When you wake up, you notice that you're here. "Here," in my case, was Pittsburgh. I put in the three rivers that meet here . . . [and] the great chain of the Alleghenies [that] kept pioneers out of Pittsburgh until the 1760's. . . . I put in Lake Erie, and summers along its mild shore. . . . I put in the pioneer who "broke wilderness," and the romance of the French and Indian Wars that centered around Fort Duquesne and Fort Pitt. . . . I put in the Scotch-Irish families who dominate Pittsburgh and always have . . . the Mellons . . . Andrew Carnegie . . . Henry Clay Frick . . . [that] peculiarly American . . . mixture of piety and acquisitiveness, that love of work. (pp. 58–60)

In addition to landscape and social and industrial history, she attempts to catch the people she moved with during childhood: her dancing school class, Pittsburgh streetcar riders doomed to their tracks on Penn Avenue, the significant differences between the inhabitants of affluent suburbs like Shadyside and Squirrel Hill and those in the black neighborhoods of Homewood and Brushton, the group that occupied the balcony of the Shadyside Presbyterian Church each Sunday to stare at the apse's mosaic of Christ, "barefoot, alone and helpless looking"—all take their peculiar animus from the settings they occupy.

Her parents, whom she lovingly describes as occupying the "lunatic fringe" of this context, also are defined in relation to Pittsburgh—sometimes in their striking difference from their more conventional peers.

> My father was a dreamer; he lived differently from other men around him. One day he abruptly quit the family firm—when I was ten—and took off down the Ohio River in a boat by himself to search out the roots of jazz in New Orleans. He came back after several months and withdrew from corporate life forever. He knew the world well—all sorts of things, which he taught us to take an interest in: how people build bridge pilings in the middle of a river, how jazz came up the river to be educated in Chicago, how the pioneers made their way westward from Pittsburgh, down the Ohio River, sitting on the tops of their barges and singing "Bang Away, My Lulu."
>
> My mother was both a thinker and what one might call a card. If she lay on the beach with friends and found the conversation dull, she would give a little push with her heel and roll away. People were stunned. She rolled deadpan and apparently effortlessly, her arms and legs extended tidily, down the beach to the distant water's edge where she lay at ease just as she had been, but half in the surf, and well out of earshot. She was not only a card but a wild card, a force for disorder. She regarded even tiny babies as straight men, and liked to step on the drawstring of a crawling baby's gown, so that the baby crawled and crawled and never got anywhere except into a little ball at the top of the gown. (pp. 63–64)

Their jokes (her mother's favorite is an extended one about the polysyllabic possibilities in the name of Giants' infielder Wayne Terwilliger who bunts in a crucial game with the Pirates) as well as their dreams (floating down the Ohio) are predicated on Pittsburgh iconography. Even the WASP boys she dated in early adolescence, boys who "wore ties from the time their mothers could locate their necks," are characterized as "Pittsburgh Presbyterian boys" (p. 92).

Historic settlers are also imagined, as well as early industry and its magnates—including the paradox of Andrew Carnegie, the U.S. Steel mogul who built "free libraries and museums and an art gallery" for the workers "at the same time he had them working sixteen hours a day, six days a week, at subhuman wages, and drinking water full of typhoid and cholera because he and other business owners opposed municipal works like water filtration plants" (p. 66).

The intention of all this "context" is ultimately to "dig deeply into the exuberant heart of a child and the restless, violent heart of an adolescent" (p. 68).

In her process of becoming fully awake Dillard writes two extended "meditations" on childhood awareness. Each hinges on an extended metaphor animated by a specific Pittsburgh locale and encapsulating a particular lesson for the child. One occurs at the age of 8 or 9 when she pits her own bodily limitations against the powers of the imagination. By a willing suspension of disbelief she convinces herself that by running faster and faster down Penn Avenue, flapping her arms more and more wildly she will, indeed, take flight. "I was running down the Penn Avenue side-walk, revving up for an act of faith. I was conscious and self-conscious. I knew well that people could not fly—as well as anyone knows it—but I also knew the kicker: that, as the books put it, with faith all things are possible."

Running up the sidewalk "full tilt," Dillard says, "I knew I was too old really to believe in this as a child would, out of ignorance; instead, I was experimenting as a scientist would, testing both the thing itself and the limits of my own courage in trying it." She "flies" past a business-suited pedestrian who "flattens himself against the brick wall" and looks away as she passes, "embarrassed evidently." "A linen-suited woman in her 50's did meet my exultant eye. . . . We converged. The woman's smiling, deep glance seemed to read my own awareness from my face. . . . We passed on the sidewalk with the look of accomplices who share a humor just beyond irony. What's a heart for?" (pp. 108–109).

Dillard decides, on the basis of this experience, that there are some things requiring "this kind of boldness" and, conversely, "I had not seen a great deal accomplished in the name of dignity, ever" (p. 109).

The other incident records her first awarenesses of age and mortality. She recounts in minute detail the fascination she and her sister feel when fingering the loose skin on the tops of adult hands.

Mother let me play with one of her hands. She laid it flat on a living-room end-table beside her chair. I picked up a transverse pinch of skin over the knuckle of her index finger and let it drop. The pinch didn't snap back; it lay dead across her knuckle in a yellowish ridge. I poked it; it slid intact. (p. 24)

Later, at the beach:

I felt my parent's shinbones. The bones were flat and curved, like the slats on a Venetian blind. The long edges were sharp as swords. . . . The bottoms of their toes had flattened, holding the imprint of life's smooth floors even when they were lying down. I would not let this happen to me. (p. 26)

The "flying" trope and the "loose skin" trope extend their meanings into text without requiring Dillard to chronicle childhood's stages of growth, awarenesses of age, losses of innocence. Dillard's childhood truths, how one "flies" boldly while still "rooted in the earth" or what transcends aging and dying, are recognizable "axial lines" to any reader familiar with *Pilgrim at Tinker Creek* or *Tickets to a Prayer Wheel*.

Since "I myself was both observer and observable, and so a possible object of my own humming awareness" (p. 12), Dillard positions both herself and her reader at the hub of awareness in *An American Childhood*. This reflexive strategy, in effect watching the narrator watching herself learn, serves to intensify the reader's participation in the text.

Kate Simon uses a very similar technique in *Bronx Primitive* (1982) and its sequel *A Wider World* (1986)—narratives that may differ in land-scape, detail, and the requirements for childhood survival, but that also display a narrator setting her childhood in motion through images while simultaneously assessing it. Simon creates a "neighborhood," a compos-ite of place and people—Lafontaine Avenue in the Bronx, the crucible in which the "I" is forged. Simon's story emerges from a culture more ethnic and diverse than Dillard's—where beliefs, customs, superstitions, as well as values shape the young child. To live at "2029 Lafontaine . . . [in] a row of five-story tenements that ended in a hat factory" in the years just after World War I, was to occupy an immigrant neighborhood largely composed of Irish, Italians, and Polish, Russian, and German Jews.

Bathgate, moving southward from Tremont toward Claremont Parkway, was the market street where mothers bought yard goods early in the week, as well as dried mushrooms and shoelaces. On Wednesdays they bought chick-ens and live fish to swim in the bathtub until Friday, when they became gefilte fish. Most women plucked their own chickens. A few aristocrats, like my mother and Mrs. Horowitz (who spoke English perfectly, the only Jewish woman we knew who did), paid a little dark bundle in a dusty red wig ten cents to pluck fast, her hand like the needle of a sewing machine, up down, up down, as a red and black and white garden of feathers spread at her feet. (p. 3)

As in Dillard's writing, Simon's descriptions of place, the details of Yiddish life in *Bronx Primitive*, create the particular context in which the "I" awakens.

It was in the kitchen that we learned to understand Yiddish from my father's accounts of union news read from the socialist paper, the *Freiheit*. My mother read from the *Jewish Daily Forward* the heartbreaking stories gathered in the "Bintel Brief" (bundle of letters) that wept of abandoned wives, of "Greene Cousines," spritely immigrant girls who were hanky-pankying with the eldest sons of households, set to marry rich girls and become famous doctors. The stories moved me deeply, as all stories of betrayal and abandonment did, while my mother laughed. We loved to watch her laugh, big tears rolling down her face as the laughter rocked her plump body back and forth, but I found her humor chilling, heartless. She told one laughing story that appalled me for years: there was a man who could neither sit nor stand nor lie down (this with elaborations of voice and gesture), so he found a solution—he hanged himself. Another story concerned an old man who had trouble peeing—great effort and pain contorted her face and body—and consulted a doctor for relief. The doctor asked the man how old he was. Eighty-three. "Well," said the doctor, "you've peed enough. Go home, old man." We were constantly told to respect the old; here she was being amused by a sick old man. It wasn't until I picked up the fatalistic ironies of Jewish humor that I understood and almost forgave her the cruel jokes.

. . . The end room was my parents' bedroom with its big bed, chest of drawers, and my mother's talented sewing machine. Her feet rocking the treadle that said in metal letters "Singer," her hand smoothing the material taut as the needle chased her fingers, the turning, turning spool of thread feeding the jumping needle were a stunning show. Equally remarkable were the narrow long drawers, three on each side of the machine. You pulled a knob and out came long open boxes full of papers of shining, meticulously spaced pins, empty spools to string as trains, full spools that spilled baby rainbows, bits of silk and matte cotton to mix and match in myriad combinations, the dull with the shiny, the yellow with the blue, the white with the red, the square with the round; endless. Whether it was because of the dignity of the parental bed or the multitude of treasures in the sewing machine, it was in this room that my brother and I played most peaceably, most happily, a room I still see. . . . The fire escape was our viewing balcony down on the eventful lot we shared with Monterey Avenue, and it became our minute bedroom on hot nights when we slept folded on each other tight as petals on a bud, closed from the perilous stairs by a high board. (p. 4)

Simon slowly opens the petals on this bud by tracing their actual immigration, a journey from Warsaw to America when she was 4, accompanied by her mother and sickly 2½-year-old brother.

> We left for America. My brother was two and a half, a babbler in several languages, a driven entertainer and flirt. His arms and hands were weak but usable, his legs not at all; he moved with amazing, mischievous rapidity by shuffling on his behind when he wasn't being carried. I was four, grown silent and very capable. I could lift him to the pot, clean him, and take him off. I could carry him to bed and mash his potato. I knew where he might bump his head, where he might topple, how to divert him when he began to blubber. It was a short childhood. I had my first baby at not quite four, better trained in maternal wariness and responsibility than many fully grown women I later observed. At four I also knew one could intensely love and as intensely hate the being who was both core and pit of one's life. (p. 21)

Envisioning America, in *A Wider World*, as "the land where Papa is" and the land of "beautiful oranges and big white eggs" that will cure her brother's rickets, Simon becomes "a citizen of Lafontaine . . . a watcher with many eyes, a listener with many ears, a hider in shadows wearing soundless shoes to spy out the wonders of the bizarre, multitongued worlds of my subjects" (p. 3).

Her watchful intensity is fueled sometimes by curiosity and sometimes by fear: fear of being discovered "unclean" by the school nurse, fear that her rallying brother will sicken once again and die, fear of dropping her baby sister when carrying her down the perilous fire escape stairs, fear of an authoritative father who forces her to practice the piano hours a day, living out the fantasy that she will have a concert career.

> There was nothing to do with the fears but give them a companion courage, a courage that early learned slyness and exasperating silence, silence that enraged my father, who liked shrieking combat. . . . My mother, from whom I had learned the vengeful strength of silences, understood mine, and tacitly approved of them. I was her defiance of the gods that brought her from an amusing and lucrative career in Warsaw to scrubbing floors and peeling potatoes in a provincial place called the Bronx. It was from her, her determination to attend daily English classes in the local library and meet with her mandolin group one night a week in spite of my father's sour remarks, that I began to know the face of courage that was independence. (p. 4)

Bronx Primitive and *A Wider World* chronicle the growth of this "independence" via a series of images that both recreate the experience and retrospectively comment on it. The reader is never far from the awareness of

Simon looking back, separating from the experiential flow of the tumbling years to record what is of the greatest significance, what, in her phrase, "counts." But what remains in the memory are the shimmering images: the kitchen, the "talented" Singer, the fire escape, the English class at the local library: All stand as portals to a new world.

Memories that cut through ordinary and trivializing experience, making some moments in our personal history stand out as if in *bas relief*, form the content of Mary Lee Settle's "London—1944," (1988). Opening the essay with this rhetorical question, "How do I capture a city and a time?" Settle begins by suggesting that many who lived wartime experience needed some means of communicating its significance. Without these exchanges "one friend who brought back a hidden wound of one forever relived day was shot himself nearly forty years later" (p. 1). The trigger that presses her to discharge her "significant insight" comes at an innocuous dinner party in New York 18 months after she comes home from the war. That incident she saves for the end of the essay. Sandwiched between the need to describe the war and the responsibility to bear witness to what she sees as the significance of her experience are a series of vignettes of 1944 in London, where Settle spent 10 months, at first on sick leave from the WAAF of the RAF. Clearly, her method differs from Dillard's and Simon's in two respects: The author remains in a fixed position, looking back at a moment in history rather than reactivating it in a "continuous present"; second, she has an historical obligation to discharge—one that feels as pressing to her as any personal subtexts.

Part of her writer's intention is to de-mythicize the war-torn city from "the over-simple pictures of courage and love" gleaned from movies and nostalgic war correspondents' accounts of the time. She wishes to "wipe clean with recall" the London she encountered, and she uses sensory detail and a series of brief meetings with knots of people involved in the war effort to accomplish this.

> Osbert Sitwell wrote that the blackout made a medieval city of London. It didn't. There were no pine torches, no wax tapers shining through windows to defeat the darkness. Instead, it was the opposite. London was plunged into the terrible present century and lay exposed under an open, dangerous sky. The pitch darkness was inside of rooms, as if they were caves deep underground before the blackout curtains were drawn and the lamps were lit.
>
> Outside, in the street, London became country again under a changing sky. The buildings were dark monoliths; the streets canyons between cliffs. There were snaggled bombed-out gaps in the townhouse rows that let the moonlight in through high windows that had once been private rooms, here a fragment of wallpaper with faded rain-streaked animals of a nursery, there

a drunken toilet, still clinging to the wall. Many of the ancient churches were only ruins that looked like stone lace that etched the night sky. During the blitz they had been low on the priorities of the fire fighters.

To new arrivals in London, it seemed pitch black out of doors, too, but not, by 1943, to Londoners. People had become conscious again of the phases of the moon, the light from stars. They had regained their country eyes. The darkness was full of noises, the echo of footsteps, of people talking, the cries for taxis. Sound itself seemed amplified and dependable in the half-blindness of the street. The smell was of dust, of damp plaster in the air, and of the formaldehyde scent of the smoke from dirty coal that lodged in the yellow fog. The stained sandbags, the rust, the dull, peeling paint, damp that made great dark lines down the walls, made London seem like a long-neglected, leaky attic.

It was fear that was medieval, and largely unadmitted to this day, fear of the full moon, the bomber's moon, as our ancestors had shrunk from its insane light and the cry of the wolf. (pp. 2–3)

Since "recovery" from signals shock occurred quickly to the WAAF's satisfaction, Settle is taken off sick leave and, in lieu of rejoining her group, reports for service at the American Office of War Information.

There were fine editors, good writers, movie actors, poets, in the halls of the OWI, and I realize now that I was as glamorous to them as they were to me. Somehow I had touched the war they had come to. I knew things I could tell . . . had had the experiences they had come to share. What I had learned to take for granted, service in the forces was, to them, a fascination.
. . . I was plunged straight from lorry to limousine, from the barracks to tea at the Savoy with Robert Sherwood, Alfred Lunt, and Lynn Fontanne. (p. 5)

For all their sense of privilege, Settle develops a grudging respect for these editors, writers, and film makers and their efforts to be of service. Danger makes time more valuable. The threat of violence common to their situation levels class and national distinctions. "We talked as people have not talked in England since. We talked on trains, in bars, in canteens, in Lyons Corner Houses, on buses, as if our statements had to be made before it was too late" (p. 10).

The buzz bombs made the summer miserable. They came, self-propelling bombs with little stubby wings. They looked like huge cigars, and they sounded like motorcycles in the air. The more that were shot down coming over the coast, the more came into London. We began to listen; we listened all the time, whether consciously or not, to the cutoff of the engines which meant that the buzz bomb would either crash straight down or glide. (p. 13)

Friendships made "for a sense of safety. . . . Often not true safety at all, but a psychic calm" (p. 15). And refuge found in friends forms the remaining subjects of the essay up through the Allied invasion of Normandy. Settle describes in the wind-down of the war a common phenomenon, a "crack-up at the release of pressure"—an explosion she compares with the last of Wernher von Braun's terrible weapons, "the silent, suddenly ground-erupting V2s."

"London—1944" closes by fleshing out the picture within the frame Settle initially offers as the *raison d'etre* for the essay. Setting: a dinner party in New York in the spring of 1945. The painter Constantine Alajolou is there as is Tilly Losch and "an elegant Free French officer who had been sent in his beautifully cut uniform with his beautifully cut aristocratic face as a propaganda visitor" (p. 19). His assignment, as Settle sees it, was to improve the image of France, which many in America saw as sullied by five years of occupation. His function was to "obscure the truth that many of its citizens had collaborated with Hitler or been passive under the Vichy regime" (p. 19).

"Taking for granted in the company that it was an acceptable remark," he drops the last buzz bomb. "Well, at least Hitler did one thing for us. He got rid of the Jews in France" (p. 19). Settle's shock momentarily paralyzes her and she admits, "I did not leave quickly enough. In short, I was polite" (p. 20).

Her essay is the retort she would like to have made, tardy perhaps but never too late, and paradoxically in art reaching a wider audience than had it been delivered at that dinner party. Although "the world runs on shallowness for the most part, we are left, at least, with a residue of social shame as a weapon" (p. 20).

Remembering a place, extracting its marrow, trying to make of its senselessness some sense is also the technique Joan Didion employs in "Salvador" (1983). Unable to depend on the cutting edge of anti-Semitism to sculpt her essay, however, her shocks of recognition are more ambiguously rendered in a land where nothing is clear. She hopes to use "a residue of social shame as a weapon" as she describes the dumps of human bodies, the anxiety of living in constant danger, the arbitrary hits by death squads who appear out of nowhere and execute arbitrarily, without trial. How the U.S. government with its aid and covert strategies factors into the perpetuation of this system is the unanswered question lurking in the background of most of Didion's scenarios.

Although it's hard to imagine shocking a readership already inured to the butchery of Salvador by newspaper accounts, TV journalism, and poems detailing a jar of severed ears on display in a Salvadoran Colonel's house in Carolyn Forche's "The Colonel" (1981), shock is exactly the re-action Didion's opening descriptions in "Salvador" elicit.

> Terror is the given of the place. Black-and-white police cars cruise in pairs, each with the barrel of a rifle extruding from an open window. Road-blocks materialize at random, soldiers fanning out from trucks and taking positions, fingers always on triggers, safeties clicking on and off. Aim is taken as if to pass the time. Every morning *El Diario de Hoy* and *La Prensa Grafica* carry cautionary stories. "*Una madre y sus dos hivos fueron asesinados con arma cortante (corvo) por ocho sujetos desconocidos el lunes en la noche*": A mother and her two sons hacked to death in their beds by eight *desconocidos*, unknown men. The same morning's paper: the unidentified body of a young man, strangled, found on the shoulder of a road. Same morning, different story: the unidentified bodies of three young men, found on another road, their faces partially destroyed by bayonets, one face carved to represent a cross.
>
> . . . The body count kept by what is generally referred to in San Salva-dor as "the Human Rights Commission" is higher than the embassy's, and documented periodically by a photographer who goes out looking for bod-ies. These bodies he photographs are often broken into unnatural positions, and the faces to which the bodies are attached (when they are attached) are equally unnatural, sometimes unrecognizable as human faces, obliterated by acid or beaten to a mash of misplaced ears and teeth or slashed ear to ear and invaded by insects. "*Encontrado en Antiguo Cascatlan el dia 25 de Marzo 1982: camison de dormir celeste*," the typed caption reads on one photograph: found in Antiguo Cascatlan March 25, 1982 wearing a sky-blue nightshirt. The captions are laconic. Found in Sayapango May 21, 1982. Found in Mejicanos June 11, 1982. Found at El Playon May 30, 1982, white shirt, purple pants, black shoes.
>
> The photograph accompanying that last caption shows a body with no eyes, because the vultures got to it before the photographer did. There is a special kind of practical information that the visitor to El Salvador acquires immediately, the way visitors to other places acquire information about the currency rates, the hours for the museums. In El Salvador one learns that vultures go first for the soft tissue, for the eyes, the exposed genitalia, the open mouth. One learns that an open mouth can be used to make a specific point, can be stuffed with something emblematic; stuffed, say, with a penis, or, if the point has to do with land title, stuffed with some of the dirt in question. One learns that hair deteriorates less rapidly than flesh, and that a skull surrounded by a perfect corona of hair is a not uncommon sight in the body dumps. (p. 630)

Unable to stop noticing even though apprehension and anxiety began to fatigue her and dull the sharp edges of dismay, she and her husband move from native hotels, the Camino Real and the Presidente, to the Hotel

Sheraton. Despite being surrounded by "bars of Camay and Johnson's baby soap, crushed ice and Coca-Cola," she is acutely aware of the fact the "hotel has figured rather too prominently in certain local stories involving the disappearance and death of Americans" (p. 635). Sniffing for the stench of American collusion, Didion constructs this intricate web of possible connections.

> It was at the Sheraton that one of the few American *desaparecidos*, a young free-lance writer named John Sullivan, was last seen, in December of 1980. It was also at the Sheraton, after eleven on the evening of January 3, 1981, that the two American advisers on agrarian reform, Michael Hammer and Mark Pearlman, were killed, along with the Salvadoran director of the Institute for Agrarian Transformation, Jose Rodolfo Viera. The three were drinking coffee in a dining room off the lobby, and whoever killed them used an Ingram MAC-10, without sound suppressor, and then walked out through the lobby, unapprehended. The Sheraton has even turned up in the investigation into the December 1980 deaths of the four American churchwomen, Sisters Ita Ford and Maura Clarke, the two Maryknoll nuns; Sister Dorothy Kazel, the Ursuline nun; and Jean Donovan, the lay volunteer. In *Justice in El Salvador: A Case Study*, prepared and released in July of 1982 in New York by the Lawyers' Committee for International Human Rights, there appears this note:

>> "On December 19, 1980, the [Duarte government's] Special Investigative Commission reported that 'a red Toyota 3/4-ton pickup was seen leaving (the crime scene) at about 11:00 p.m. on December 2' and that 'a red splotch on the burned van' of the churchwomen was being checked to determine whether the paint splotch 'could be the result of a collision between that van and the red Toyota pickup.' By February 1981, the Maryknoll Sisters' Office of Social Concerns, which has been actively monitoring the investigation, received word from a source which it considered reliable that the FBI had matched the red splotch on the burned van with a red Toyota pickup belonging to the Sheraton hotel in San Salvador. . . . Subsequent to the FBI's alleged matching of the paint splotch and a Sheraton truck, the State Department has claimed, in a communication with the families of the churchwomen, that 'the FBI could not determine the source of the paint scraping.'"

> There is also mention in this study of a young Salvadoran businessman named Hans Christ (his father was a German who arrived in El Salvador at the end of World War II), a part owner of the Sheraton. Hans Christ lives now in Miami, and that his name should have even come up in the Maryknoll investigation made many people uncomfortable, because it was Hans Christ, along with his brother-in-law, Ricardo Sol Meza, who, in April of 1981, was first charged with the murders of Michael Hammer and Mark Pearlman and

Jose Rodolfo Viera at the Sheraton. These charges were later dropped, and were followed by a series of other charges, arrests, releases, expressions of "dismay" and "incredulity" from the American embassy, and even, in the fall of 1982, confessions to the killings from two former National Guard corporals, who testified that Hans Christ had led them through the lobby and pointed out the victims. (pp. 635–636)

Unable to shake the eerie feeling of being watched, of possible covert activity everywhere, Didion notices the bullet marks remaining on the hotel walls where the "hit" took place and later "shadowy silhouettes" behind the windows of a Cherokee Chief parked outside their room and even later, a "shadow crouched between the pumps at the Esso station next door, carrying a rifle" (p. 636). She and her husband, the only people sitting on the front porch and at a table illuminated by a candle, fight the impulse to run. "We continued talking, carefully. Nothing came of this, but I did not forget the sensation of having been in a single instant demoralized, undone, humiliated by fear, which is what I meant when I said that I came to understand in El Salvador the mechanism of terror" (p. 636).

When Didion is about to leave she visits a huge shopping center, the Metro Center, replete with designer jeans, Bloomingdale's towels, Stolich-naya vodka, and background Muzak featuring "I Left My Heart in San Fran-cisco" and "American Pie" (with its ironic "singing this will be the day that I die" refrain).

> This was a shopping center that embodied the future for which El Sal-vador was presumably being saved, and I wrote it down dutifully, this being the kind of "color" I knew how to interpret, the kind of inductive irony, the detail that was supposed to illuminate the story. As I wrote it down I real-ized that I was no longer much interested in this kind of irony, that this was a story that would not be illuminated by such details, that this was a story that would perhaps not be illuminated at all, that this was perhaps even less a "story" than a true *noche obscura* [dark night]. As I waited to cross back over the Boulevard de los Heroes to the Camino Real I noticed soldiers herding a young civilian into a van, their guns at the boy's back, and I walked straight ahead, not wanting to see anything at all. (p. 637)

If Settle catches the "banality of evil" in her descriptions of the French officer's offhand remark of ridding France of the Jews, delivered in the "safe context" of the New York City fashionable dinner party after the war, Didion's evil is one crackling with kinetic energy, threatening to break out in the present, anywhere, without provocation or a thread of logic. And if Settle can at least target "the enemy," uncovering even well-domesticated versions of intolerance and bigotry, Didion finds the enemy unknowable, indistinguishable from its victims—cloaked in *noche obscura*, a dark night of the soul, which in all its impenetrability defeats her attempts at assessment. That very impenetrability becomes her real subject.

Maxine Kumin, the writer who first came to mind as a practitioner of Morrison's "emotional memory," describes in her "A Sense of Place," in the essay collection *In Deep* (1987), how a "sense of place underwritten by private history is a part of the natural order of things" (p. 150). Hers is not a global canvas, but a small, intensely rendered corner of the world. Describing her early morning animal tending and feeding rituals on her New Hampshire farm is a way for her to create in her writerly mind "alert time, newly wakened" and so to begin her artistic as well as pragmatical duties of the day.

> It's madness, this glut of critters to look after, but it is a glut of shared needs. They need me as custodian of their confined lives, and I need them in a variety of ways—aesthetic, maternal, and some inchoate, perhaps indecipherable ways, all bound up in this matter of influence—influence of region, place, idea.
>
> I cannot imagine myself living, as a writer, outside New England. When I am away from the farm, locked up in motels or hotels into which no outside air may come without the intervention of machinery; when I am on the road for poe-biz and must eat Styrofoam airline breakfasts and cardboard airline lunches, I can stand back from this life and raise up some comments about it. What Louise Bogan called "subliminal mewings, roarings and retchings, on odd scraps of paper" come out of these forays into the world, falling often onto the backs of boarding passes. Eventually these jottings may work out as poems on my desk in my study, a narrow little upstairs room that looks out onto the winding dirt road below.
>
> Nor is it quite true that I cannot write away from home. Of course I can. I have on occasion written fiercely fast and even immodestly well when put on hold in a distant country, a poet-in-residence, for instance, in Pennsylvania or Maryland or Florida. I can, in fact, see my place, my hardscrabble kingdom on a hill, more clearly from a distance. I have forgotten in what anonymous motel, in a brown room smelling of old cigars, I wrote the first draft of the following poem. I know that it was winter and I was acutely, guiltily homesick and the overwhelming helpless admission of our own mortality visited me there. I know too that a New England winter is the very archetype of winters, and that winter itself signifies in the Jungian scheme of things, in the collective unconscious, the final phase, the end of sentience. So the poem conscripts all its forces to outlast the season.

Feeding Time

Sunset. I pull on
parka, boots, mittens, hat,
cross the road to the paddock.
Cat comes,
the skinny, feral tom
who took us on last fall.
Horses are waiting.
Each enters his box
in the order they've all
agreed on, behind my back.
Cat supervises from the molding cove.
Hay first. Water next. Grain last.
Check thermometer: seven degrees.
Check latches. Leave

The sky
goes purple, blotched with red.
Feed dog next.
I recross the road to the woodshed.
Snappish moment with cat
but no real contest.
Wag, wag, kurchunk! The plate
is polished. Dog
grovels his desire
to go inside, like a log
by the fire.

Two above.
Above, it's gray
with meager afterglow.
Feed birds next.
I wade by way
of footprint wells through deep snow
to cylinders on trees.

Cat follows
observing distribution
of sunflower seeds.
Checks out each heel-toe
I've stepped in, in case
something he needs,
something small and foolish lurks.
No luck.

Penultimate,
cat gets
enormous supper:
chicken gizzards! Attacks
these like a cougar
tearing, but not in haste.
Retires to barn loft
to sleep in the hay,
or pretends to. Maybe
he catches dessert this way.

Now us,
Dear one. My soup, your bread
in old blue bowls that have withstood
thirty years of slicings and soppings.
Where are the children
who ate their way through helpings
of cereals and stews
to designs of horse, pig,
sheep on view
at the bottom of the dish?
Crying, *when I grow up,*
children have got their wish.

It's ten below.
The house dozes.
The attic stringers cough.
Time that blows on the kettle's rim
waits to carry us off.

Clearly, the impulse for poems is here for me, in the vivid turn of the seasons, in the dailiness of growing things, in the quite primitive satisfaction of putting up vegetables and fruits, gathering wild nuts and mushrooms, raising meat for the table, collecting sap for sweetening. Without religious faith and without the sense of primal certitude that faith brings, I must take my only comfort from the natural order of things. (pp. 159–162)

As time and the continuity of memory captured in a particular place unroll its tape for Kumin, she becomes conscious of how she and her husband, in clearing and making fertile a particular tract of land, have not only nurtured themselves, but joined a long line of stewards of this land. This activity, she suspects sadly, is coming to an end. "There is not one full-time farmer left in my community. . . . Agribusiness had made it impossible to sustain a family any longer, for example, on a herd of thirty Holsteins" (p. 165). And while she is too tough-minded to simply castigate agribusiness or sentimentalize the family farm, she laments the loss of a stable population of family farms in New England for "most of all it meant that human beings still felt some connection to and responsibility for the animal lives and land in their keeping" (p. 148). This is a crucial loss to Kumin. Since animals "are my confederates . . . they are rudimentary and untiring and changeless, where we are sophisticated, weary and fickle, they make me better than I am." If we lose this kind of connection, she argues, "we will also lose our ability to respond in humane and significant ways to our surroundings" (p. 168).

In another essay, "Wintering Over," in the collection *To Make a Prairie* (1979), Kumin casts herself as an anonymous observer to an encounter between her grown son and daughter. "A woman creeps on all fours through a squash patch in mid-September seeking out the last bloomers" (p. 163). From the safety of her ground-level peep-sight she sees the spaghetti squash she has come to pick, her son "rattling up the hill in his ten-year old Dodge" (p. 163), and her mare—a few years ago "a dangerous runaway." Still employing the neutrality of the third person, she watches her son's arrival.

> When the boy comes up the hill in his red Dodge Dart this September morning it is to see his sister, visiting from Europe where she lives. She is three years his senior and from the time he crept across the kitchen floor to paddle in the dog's water dish and she retrieved him, they have had a mythic bond. Now he is six feet tall, elegantly slender, with the sky-blue eyes of a newborn. A handle-bar mustache mutes the fullness of his lower lip while giving his face a gently melancholic, if not world-weary air. He is twenty-two. His sister, although gracefully constructed, is five feet, one inch. So much for genetic similarities.
>
> The mother watches them embrace. Camouflaged, she can afford to conduct some meticulous noticing. They are perfect with their four arms and four legs of mismatched lengths, and their laughter overlaps perfectly. Arms entwined like school children or young lovers, they leave the sun and go indoors. (p. 166)

From her observation post, vitally connected to the "seeds" she has grown and cultivated, her mind plays over the past, focusing on all the other New England winters that marked her children's rites of passage to adulthood.

> This was the time of year he traditionally came down with the croup, the little one they wintered over so painfully those early years with the kettle

and the smell of tincture of benzoin in the room. His sister braved the steam to play checkers with him, or Fish or Old Maid. They ate Fig Newtons and the crumbs migrated between the sheets. (p. 168)

Memory parallels the unfolding of the day, just as light punctuates with its assessments. The day slowly recedes into darkness. The reader simultaneously grasps the allegory: one of mothering, of the seasons of nurturance, of letting go, all rendered "at ground level." Kumin examines the images of her world in such a patient, thoughtful way that they appear, finally, illuminated from within.

"Tell me the landscape in which you live, and I will tell you who you are," says Ortego y Gassett in a quote opening Kathleen Norris's *Dakota: A Spiritual Geography* (1993). In it Norris (a poet whose volumes *Falling Off*, 1971, and *The Middle of the World*, 1981, received wide acclaim) describes her decision to leave a literary career in New York City and return with her husband, poet David Dwyer, to assume the inheritance of her grandparents' house in South Dakota where she has lived for almost 20 years.

Her book is written as an extended metaphor, one linking the inhospitable land to the spiritual challenges and advantages one experiences in remote, silent, and often mysterious places. Among the advantages she locates are the strengths of a people situated "at the point of transition between east and west in America, geographically and psychically isolated from either coast, and unlike either the Midwest or the desert west" (p. 7).

Living in such a landscape, experiencing a sense of emotional as well as geographical remoteness, teaches her to *notice*: "a story telling tradition" shared by Plains people . . . Native Americans . . . and monks (p. 6); the language of farmers, "as eloquent as it is grammatically unorthodox" (p. 19); the "miraculous little things" available to one removed from cities and enveloped in the "near-absence of human noise."

The way native grasses spring back from a drought, greening before your eyes; the way a snowy owl sits on a fencepost, or a golden eagle hunts, wings outstretched over grassland that seems to go on forever. Pelicans rise noisily from a lake; an antelope stands stock-still, its tattooed neck like a message in unbreakable code; columbines, their long stems beaten down by hail, bloom in the mud, their whimsical and delicate flowers intact. (p. 10)

Such exercises in concrete language are good calisthenics for the poet Norris wisely observes; they are also, as the inner logic of the book documents, exercises for the soul. How the Plains have not only been essential to her "growth as a writer" but also "formed [her] spiritually" (p. 11) is at the heart of what she uncovers. Not only does she begin a formal relationship with the Benedictines "as an oblate, or associate," but she realizes the Plains "themselves have become my monastery," a genuine surprise to "a married woman, thoroughly Protestant, who often has more doubt than anything resembling faith" (p. 17).

As she describes the dailiness of her life as a poet-in-residence in the schools and a bookkeeper for her and her husband's brief venture into the cable television business (an investment "buying them three years of writing time")—the difficulties of living and teaching in communities that cannot "hold the best of their young," the resentments and mistrust that greet any "outsider"—she stumbles "on a basic truth of asceticism."

> . . . it is a way of surrendering to reduced circumstances in a manner that enhances the whole person. It is a radical way of knowing exactly who, what, and where you are in defiance of those powerful forces in society—alcohol, drugs, television, shopping malls, motels—that aim to make us forget. (p. 23)

In *Dakota*, Norris alternates between bare-bones narrative, exemplum-like in its simplicity, and short tone poems designed to evoke the abiding presence of the holy as it is embedded within and released from the ordinary. Reading *Dakota* is analogous to driving along unrelieved stretches of Plains highway and, upon topping a little rise in the road, happening onto a sudden spring vista stretching as far as the eye can see. These vistas, rendered as lyric interludes, sing and throb with meaning.

> I'm at a hermitage in high summer. At four this morning a bird began singing in the grove; within an hour he had raised a chorus. The wind comes up, then suddenly is still, in the green flame that is this world. (p. 105)

> All Souls' blustery and chill. I hear them before I see them, six lines scribbling across the white sky. I look up at the tiny crosses beating above me. The pain is new each year, and I'm surprised, even though I expect it: the sudden cold, the geese passing over. (p. 204)

What seems remarkable to me about Kathleen Norris's poetic method of investigation is not that she frequently sees a universal mystery or truth in a concrete detail, but that she can reverse the process, decoding a symbol into its concrete applications.

> "All flesh is grass" is a hard truth, and it has real meaning for people who grow grass, cut it, bale it, and go out every day in winter to feed it to cows. They watch that grass turning into flesh, knowing that they in turn will eat it as beef. They can't pretend not to know that their flesh, too, is grass. (p. 174)

For Norris the Plains are fertile soil in which parables abound, but it is her translation of the parables that reveals her inner consciousness. If one thinks of poetic progression as composed less of continuous narration and more of highly charged moments that are linked associatively, then the structure of *Dakota* is such a progression, a kind of electric conduction that both completes the circuitry of thought and discharges the emotional voltage.

Crossing the Racial Divide: African-American Autobiography

In several recent African-American autobiographies the moment of "heightened consciousness" through which the narrators "site" their stories is shaped and pressured by public opinion. Gloria Wade-Gayles's *Pushed Back to Strength: A Black Woman's Journey Home* (1993), Lorene Cary's *Black Ice* (1991), and Charlayne Hunter-Gault's *In My Place* (1992) explore "a sense of place" that is determined by *where* and *when* they walked out of segregated America. The personal is quite literally political in these accounts: Gloria Wade-Gayles tells the story of growing up "black and female in a segregated south," Memphis in the 1940s to be specific, and coming of age during the civil rights movement in the early 1960s; Lorene Cary, a bright, ambitious teenager from Philadelphia, finds herself in 1972 transplanted into the formerly all-white, all-male environs of the elite Saint Paul's School in New Hampshire, a scholarship student in a "boot camp" for future American leaders; in January 1961, 19-year-old Charlayne Hunter passes through a gauntlet of jeering, spitting whites to become the first black woman to attend the University of Georgia. On one level then each account pivots on an historical "moment," a time of change, a reversal of racial assumptions.

From that historical moment each author uncovers another level of the story, the knotted and complex set of thoughts and feelings occasioned in her by that moment. In crossing America's racial divide each author describes the subjective realities of segregation as well as the capacities within herself to challenge it.

Gloria Wade-Gayles describes *Pushed Back to Strength* as a "narrative of rememberings" (p. viii) and, in a nonlinear way, it traces her 50 years of life. Her journey moves from the 1940s and 1950s in Memphis housing projects, through graduate school, through a marriage that fails and a second that succeeds, through the growth of two children, and finally to her current position as a nationally known professor of English at Spelman College. Destinations interest Wade-Gayles less than the inner consciousness suspended in the arrivals and departures en route. She is interested in detecting the patterns in her life, always conscious that although it is uniquely inscribed, it is also a life broadly representative of journeys taken by other sensitive, talented black people growing up in the American South in the 1940s and 1950s.

She studies her family first, keying on her mother, who pours such energy and love into her two daughters that "I grew up believing I was somebody with a special future, in spite of the fact that I lived in a low-income housing project" (p. 9). Then there is her grandmother, "Proud Nola," who scrutinizes trendy dresses in downtown department stores so that she can duplicate them at home on her foot-operated sewing machine. While she describes men in the family as "buttresses and protectors," "it was the women who gave meaning to the expression 'pushed back to strength'" (p. 13).

Nonetheless, one of the most vivid portraits is of her mother's brother, "Uncle Prince," a gifted artist and poet who inspires the teacher and performer capacities in Wade-Gayles. Unfortunately, his genius is inseparable from his drinking, a strategy he employs to defend himself against the mean streets of racism. His premature death affects Wade-Gayles profoundly, and it is through his story that she "sites" two of its lessons: first, that his life replicates a tragic pattern of destruction for thousands of black males of his generation who are unable to locate employment or educational opportunities commensurate with their talents; second, that his life and its meaning need not be wasted, but instead can be "pushed back to strength," reinvested in Wade-Gayles's son, who resembles Uncle Prince in every respect except alcoholism.

> My son, at twenty-three, wears my uncle's face. Like my uncle, he has a winning personality. He performs for the family. . . . He draws and paints. He talks race and change. My uncle was a renegade; my son is a young revolutionary. I think that my Uncle Prince has had his final homecoming in my son. (p. 55)

If the past has been tragic, the present need not simply echo it.

All the while Wade-Gayles describes her life, she also describes the second half of the twentieth century as seen through the eyes of a thoughtful, intelligent, funny, well-educated black American woman. If her book did nothing more than provide this lens on experience, it would have performed a crucial purpose, since she sees both the honor and the folly of civil rights activism. She concludes, for example, that her early admiration for her white fellow CORE workers was misplaced, since however well-intentioned the "exchanges" between CORE whites and blacks were, it was whites who invaded black territory and left: "If we were working to change whites, why didn't we work among them . . . in their communities?" (p. 130).

She explores her struggles with the black church at length: "I held on [to my religious convictions] until reason and rage convinced me to let go. . . . During the sixties I listened to Martin. During the seventies I meditated politically to the sound of Malcolm's voice on tapes that were selling on every street corner in black neighborhoods. . . . Christianity, he said, is a slave religion. I agreed with him" (p. 116). And yet in the following incantatory passage she "returns," struggling to accept a wider spiritual reality than the traditional Christianity of her Black Power days:

> They say you can't stay away for long. They say that age and marriage and motherhood pull you back from the other shore. They say that the loss of your mother will cause you to sing the old songs and to bow in prayer again to the God in whom you once believed. They say you do indeed go home again. (p. 118)

These things bring her back to a sense of the spiritual dimensions at work in her life—these things *and* her determination to live in accordance with this ethic, the only prescription for change she can endorse: "What matters is that we recognize our smallness in the universe and see kindness as the only avenue toward a larger self" (p. 120).

Returning is what brings her book full cycle, for the final chapter is devoted to recreating for her children some of the old stories, songs, games of her childhood. As these avatars of her "Old World Culture" reappear to entertain and delight her children, she underscores how even when "places have been changed beyond recognition" (p. 275), some "rememberings" ignite them again and give them life. They act as metaphors, carriers of the significances of her "journey home."

Gloria Wade-Gayles's stylistic signature is electric one-liners: a sentence or two that capture the "essence" of the person or event being described and also comment on it. Take, for example, this characterization of her distant but loving father who was physically in and out of her life, "like a train . . . returning then departing . . . [he] was a joyous melody sung at high pitch" (p. 12). Or consider the way she summarizes her family's refusal to be "head-dropping, side-stepping, yassiring, submissive colored folks" (p. 139). "Like most black people, they observed the rules just enough to stay alive. But in small, often brave ways, they walked outside the narrow circle of humiliation for blacks expertly drawn by whites" (p. 139). Or this: "My friends are too nice to be white people." Or finally this, which identifies both the method and theme of her account. Speaking of what her children may have gleaned from the stories of "her people" relayed to them before bed each night, she says: "I hope they learned that . . . culture comes from the soul of a people . . . and that some things reappear when the poofs of smoke clear. They might appear in different forms, but they come back" (p. 275).

If Wade-Gayles's account achieves its authority through cyclical return and cumulative validation, Charlayne Hunter-Gault jars the reader with a tight, concentrated focus. Most of her account details her preparation for and entrance into the previously segregated University of Georgia, the trial that ensued, and reactions to the "new reality" of court-ordered desegregation of public schools.

Like Wade-Gayles, Charlayne Hunter had a mother who convinced her *she was somebody*, an unshakable self-esteem she calls the "Queen" in herself. It is this capacity, she suggests half-humorously, that allows her to withstand the taunts and racial insults that greet her and attempt to keep her, as her title underscores, "in my place." She observes ruefully:

> . . . the notion that I was a queen took up residence in my head and was nurtured by my family and community to such an extent that, by the time I got to the University of Georgia, it was inconceivable that I might be the "nigger" they were talking about. (p. 3)

Her mother, light-skinned, sensitive, underscored her daughter's desire for a good education. Her father, tall, dark, and dramatic, was an African Methodist Episcopal minister, a denomination established in 1819 by Richard Allen. "Allen, a former slave, broke with the methodist church over their insistence that Blacks sit in seats separated from the whites . . . Allen is widely credited with starting the first protest movement by Negroes in America . . . the first attempt on the part of Negroes to strike for dignity and respect" (p. 30). All of her early chapters are orchestrated so as to suggest the inevitability of her moment in history, the crossroads of identity, time, and will.

Her father's Korean War chaplaincy takes the family to a variety of locations—Atlanta, Florida, Alaska—all of which offer forums in racial separation or commingling for the young Charlayne. By the time she reaches college age she has identified her career goal—journalism—as well as those schools (mostly white) that had journalism programs. Since Georgia has a journalism school as well as in-state aid for residents, she thinks briefly about attending, then opts for Wayne State in Detroit.

Meanwhile, the civil rights movement in Georgia is building with riveting intensity in 1959–1960. When she returns to Georgia during spring break, her friends have drafted a document protesting the "discriminatory conditions under which the Negro is living today in Atlanta." This document, delivered by 4,000 marching students of the "Atlanta University Center Colleges Coalition," announces "our time has come" (p. 143).

It is the detailed description of that time, beginning with targeting Rich's, the moderate-to-upscale department store in Atlanta that discriminated against blacks, and continuing to her entrance into the University of Georgia the following year, that forms the burning center of this account. Hunter-Gault describes the processes of entering and registering at the university with the crisp, cool style of the good journalist she is. Tellingly, she also records her inner voices, the ones that buoyed her throughout the struggle, "the voices of my grandmother reciting the Twenty-third Psalm . . . and of Nina Simone and her friends, who soothed and comforted me with 'He's Got the Whole World in His Hands' and 'Try a Little Tenderness'" (p. 201).

Her account ends with a kind of reprise of those inner voices, since 25 years later she is invited back to the University of Georgia to deliver the graduation address. Although by now she is known to millions of Americans as the national correspondent for PBS's MacNeil/Lehrer News Hour, she uses the occasion to talk about memory. Quoting Santayana's admonition that "those who cannot remember the past are doomed to repeat it," she reminds her audience what had to be done in 1961 and what has to be done today.

Lorene Cary's *Black Ice* starts with a brief retrospective, a short chapter entitled "June 1989" that contextualizes the rest of her account. Describing the joyous rites of graduation day at St. Paul's School as they unfold, she confides: "Fifteen years before I had walked down the same aisle as a graduate, and nine years later as a teacher. Now I was ending my term as a Trustee" (p. 3).

One might expect that such obvious success validated the "experiment" of integration at St. Paul's, and yet her volume starts with the recollections graduation day prompts, the burden of her own doubts and fears as a student at St. Paul's.

> I remembered the self-loathing, made worse by a poised bravado . . . I remembered duty and obligation—to my family, to the memory of dead relatives, to my people. And I remembered confusion: was it true that these teachers expected less of me than of my white peers? Or had I mistaken kindness for condescension? Were we black kids a social experiment? If we failed (or succeeded too well) would they call us off? Were we imported to help round out the white kids' education? Did it make any difference if we were? (p. 5)

Her account is constructed, in part, to explore these questions—to arrive at some consensus in her own mind as to what her St. Paul's experience has meant. In reclaiming the meaning of her history she also serves those black students who follow her to schools like St. Paul's, who begin by thinking of such opportunities as "white places where they were trespassing" and who end by remembering "this is my life . . . [not] an aberration" (pp. 5–6). She wishes to join her account to other narratives that "talked honestly about growing up black in America. I am writing this book to become part of that unruly conversation, and to bring my experience back to the community of minds that made it possible" (p. 6).

That community of minds includes Mrs. Evans, a black retired teacher in Lorene Cary's Philadelphia neighborhood who excitedly reports one day that "a very exclusive boarding school" has recently gone co-ed and is interested in "finding black girls" who are qualified to attend.

To Mrs. Evans she adds her parents—two people who, although in quite different ways, could each "fill the room" with the "intensity of their presence" (p. 15), and the black recruiters who interview and assess hopeful black students, recommending a few for on-campus interviews.

Her account arrives at its real subject when she interviews at St. Paul's. From the moment Lorene Cary "invades that space," the reader is never free of the consciousness that DuBois called double-vision, the seeing of the world twice: once as the typical adolescent struggle of a bright, achieving young woman, and once through the eyes of a black woman, sensitive to the judgments of her white assessors, sensitive to the obligations she feels she owes to her immediate family and to her race.

Set on a New England campus that looks like a Hallmark card, *Black Ice* explores Lorene's most persistent worry: that the "experiment" to integrate St. Paul's was predicated on the notion that the black students would survive, but never excel. She decides to go for straight honors.

Her academic achievements alternate with experiences common to adolescence: early experiments with love-making, painful alliances and genuine friendships, episodes of smoking dope, drinking, sneaking out after hours. These routine threats are eclipsed by the larger dangers Cary senses at St. Paul's—the rare and elusive slippery slopes she identifies with the metaphor of "black ice."

And although she graduates with honors, winning the Rector's Award at St. Paul's, goes on to receive a BA and MA from Penn, returns to teach at the school, marries, has a daughter, the consciousness of black ice, of falling when you least expect it, never leaves her.

"I have never skated on black ice," she concludes, "but perhaps my children will. They'll know it, at least, when it appears" (p. 238). In converting the metaphor from one of impending danger—a trap—to a smooth surface on which one can fly, Cary signals her hope for the future. Her account is one such smooth surface, a medium on which others can skate, hopefully less impeded than she by fears of falling.

The Oral Tradition: Native American and Chicana Autobiography

If metaphor functions in part to retrieve and preserve *collective* memory in African-American autobiography, Native American autobiography and

Chicana autobiography, grounded as they are in oral traditions, use meta-phor, writes Tey Diana Rebolledo (1990), to "fill in the gaps, one genera-tion to another, one century to another . . . to fill in the lacunas, connecting past and present" (p. 350). *Storyteller* by Leslie Marmon Silko and *Border-lands* by Gloria Anzaldua require us to widen our definitions of "metaphor," "memory," and "site"; we must replace the presumption of *literary* inten-tion, Bataille and Sands (1984) observe, with stories, poems, gossip, tradi-tional tales evoking "the way memory works" (p. 139).

Silko's collection of traditional tribal stories, poetry, short stories, and photographs, entitled *Storyteller*, uses "multigenre" forms of expression to explore memories central to the identity of Laguna Pueblo Indians. Kath-leen Mullen Sands (1992) characterizes this process as a strategy derived from the writers' stance both inside and outside the "cultures and events they narrate, profoundly affected by their experiences in non-Native cul-ture, but consistent in their expression of Native sensibilities and stories" (p. 283).

In *Storyteller* (1981) Silko uses personal narrative as no more or no less important to collective cultural memory than the other fragments, sto-ries, and tales that make up the whole. The reader is asked to uncover the connections among the "fragments," to see how personal identity reflects collective identity, to see how an autobiographical story coexists with or, as Silko puts it, "*becomes* fiction and poetry" (as quoted in Bataille & Sands, 1984, p. 139).

Silko begins *Storyteller* with a poem about her Aunt Susie, the writer and storyteller who shaped Silko's skills as a narrator.

> As with any generation
> the oral tradition depends upon each person
> listening and remembering a portion
> and it is together—
> all of us remembering what we have heard together
> that creates the whole story
> the long story of the people.
> I remember only a small part.
> But this is what I remember. (pp. 6–7)

Autobiography, then, that portion of the "whole story" which each one contributes, is interwoven into the collective story, a process using myths, tales, and photos that reshapes oral forms into written forms. Silko blends personal recollections with communal ones, sometimes collapsing time and blurring distinctions between myth and history, I and Other. Her effect is to recover patterns and from those patterns to demonstrate coherence: of past and present, of myth and history, of the individual and the communal.

For example, in *Storyteller* Silko employs several Yellow Woman stories derived from the oral tradition. The Yellow Woman stories cluster around a central theme and often feature particular characters in identifiable roles. Yellow Woman's presence signifies womanhood (the color yellow), and, depending on the context in which she appears, her stories involve abduction, isolation, or exile from the community. The community that restores her to her proper place may prosper. Silko's own rendering of the story involves a modern female narrator's abduction and captivity by a young man, Silva, who persuades her to ride toward Mexico. En route they encounter a white rancher who accuses them of rustling cattle. In the confusion and gunfire that ensue, the narrator escapes, gradually making her way back to her tribal home. Her return, like her abduction, is both real and dreamy. Silva, who originally appeared beside the river like some mythic figure of temptation, "will come back sometime and be waiting again by the river." And the narrator, who returns home to a flesh and blood husband and child, is also an emanation of Yellow Woman, adding the significance of her journey to the cumulative coherence of the Yellow Woman stories.[1]

Silko also treats the myth of Yellow Woman comically in the poem "Storytelling," by spinning the stories of three contemporary extramarital flings, as narrated by women who try to explain away their affairs as "abductions." By accretion, then, Yellow Woman comes to represent both the powerlessness of the abducted woman and the power of romance to trigger "escape"; the tragic history of a people abducted and captivated by others, and the wily resourcefulness that allows them to manipulate victim psychology.

Silko's imaginative interplay among voices, genres, myths, and histories creates a new way to "site" what one "remembers" and in the process expands our notions of memory and metaphor. Too often, ways of knowing get plotted into categories of Western theory: for example, narratology's identification of a dominant narrator who controls and gives shape to the discourse, or notions of metaphor as implied comparisons in *literary* discourse. Such categories can fool us into assuming one culture's structures are universal, or that the graphing of one sense of "self" is somehow transferable, like a stencil, to another. Leslie Marmon Silko's *Storyteller* reminds us that "you don't have anything if you don't have the stories" and that when the stories are allowed to speak in all their multiple voices, we are in touch with what informs, defines, influences the "selves" we become and the choices we make. Silko's *Storyteller* invites us to become wider, deeper repositories of alternative stories, less "knowers of narrow selves."[2]

The invitation to cross the "borders" into another consciousness, to explore cultural territory other than one's indigenous culture, is Gloria Anzaldua's point of departure in *Borderlands/La Frontera: The New Mestiza* (1987). She uses the terms in her title as representations both of physical zones and of cultural and racial and class consciousness.

> The actual physical borderland that I'm dealing with in this book is the Texas–US Southwest/Mexican border. The psychological borderlands, the sexual borderlands and the spiritual borderlands are not particular to the Southwest. In fact, the Borderlands are physically present whenever two or more cultures edge each other, where people of different races occupy the same territory, where under, lower, middle and upper classes touch, where the space between two individuals shrinks with intimacy. (p. 1, preface)

As a "border woman" Anzaldua wishes to explore the contradictions and compensations one experiences by living "on borders" and "in margins": the "unique positionings consciousness takes at these confluent streams." Her text, like Silko's, includes poems, essays, tales, and personal narratives, which are written in language that mixes Castillian Spanish with English and with "Tex-Mex." She suggests that this "infant language," Chicano Spanish, is a vital cross-pollination and reflects the "juncture of cultures" it bespeaks. She asks her readers to "meet her halfway" in exploring the meaning of the text, an invitation she reissues in her later anthology *Making Face, Making Soul, Haciendo Caras*. Calling her technique "montage," she asks the reader to participate in the "making of meaning . . . to connect the dots, to connect the fragments" (p. xviii).

Borderlands/La Frontera uses that method which is inscribed in the hearts of teachers of creative workshops when they urge: *show, don't tell.* The volume is divided into two sections, each of which attempts to *render* experience rather than simply describing it. In the first section, "Atravesando Fronteras/Crossing Borders" she details personal autobiographical experience, including the hard life of a sharecropper father who died at 38, the mother who accepts her culture's subservience to men and yet remains strong, the rarity of her own example to leave home, seek a Ph.D., "choose" to live as a lesbian. "It's an interesting path, one that continually slips in and out of the white, the Catholic, the Mexican, the indigenous, the instincts. . . . It makes for *loqueria*, the crazies. It is a path of knowledge. . . . It is a way of balancing, of mitigating duality" (p. 19).

Running simultaneously with this narrative are two other "ways of knowing" her experience: the tracing of the historic migrations of pre-Aztec Indians from what is now the southwest United States to central Mexico and then back, centuries later, as *mestizos,* the "mixed-bloods" of Indian and Spanish Conquistadors; and the tracing of the mythic and mysterious gods and goddesses that split light into dark, good into evil, protector into avenger, primitive into Christianized. The Virgin of Guadalupe is the symbol she chooses that has the capacity to subsume all of these seeming dichotomies.

> Today, *La Virgen de Guadalupe* is the single most potent religious, political and cultural image of the Chicano/Mexicano. She, like my race, is a synthesis of the old world and the new, of the religion and culture of the two races in our psyche, the conquerors and the conquered . . . she mediates between the Spanish and Indian cultures . . . she mediates between humans and the divine . . . she is the symbol of ethnic identity and of the tolerance for ambiguity that Chicanos-Mexicanos . . . by necessity possess. (p. 30)

The second half of *Borderlands,* entitled "Echecate, the Wind" is composed of poems that, perhaps even more elliptically than in the first section, render the experience of "living at the crossroads" of culture, class, gender, race, sexuality. Anzaldua wants her reader to experience her way of seeing the world. For the minority reader, she provides a validating mirror. And for the Anglo reader, she provides an alternative way of viewing the world, one that requires switching positions—at least metaphorically—with the historically marginalized other. Her account renders the *feeling* of being alienated, the *feeling* of not belonging, the *feeling* of having concepts central to your culture or world view either dismissed or misrepresented.

She underscores this demonstration method by employing the language of her culture throughout both sections of the text. The interspersing of Spanish, English, and Mexican-American phrases, words, and syntax, reinforces the psychological space at the "borderlands" and mitigates against "silencing." If one form of silencing begins with enforcing certain linguistic standards (not simply outlawing certain forms of speech, but privileging others), her insistence in using *her* language reflects and embodies the plural personalities it articulates. As one who has experienced "multiple indoctrinations" and a "collision of cultures," Gloria Anzaldua represents the "site" of self-knowledge as a *weave,* one that resists reductions or dilutions. And until Anglo readers can experience it as such, she argues, no new consciousness is possible: We remain stranded on the shores of western categories.

The capacity to see beyond those categories, or any of the exclusive boundaries one culture, religion, or class may impose on another, she calls *La facultad.*

La facultad is the capacity to see in surface phenomena the meaning of deeper realities, to see the deep structure below the surface. It is an instant "sensing," a quick perception arrived at without conscious reasoning. It is an acute awareness mediated by the part of the psyche that does not speak, that communicates in images and symbols which are the faces of feelings, that is, behind which feelings reside/hide. The one possessing this sensitivity is excruciatingly alive to the worlds. (p. 38)

La facultad is the vantage point, the "siting point," Anzaldua employs in *Borderlands*, and it is surely that capacity she hopes to hone in others who seek to give voice to what she terms a "new consciousness." Characteristically, Anzaldua renders her position in one elongated analogy.

Indigenous like corn, like corn, the *mestiza* is a product of crossbreeding, designed for preservation under a variety of conditions. Like an ear of corn— a female seed-bearing organ—the *mestiza* is tenacious, tightly wrapped in the husks of her culture. Like kernels she clings to the cob; with thick stalks and strong brace roots, she holds tight to the earth—she will survive the crossroads. (p. 81)

When Toni Morrison describes her need to supply, uncover, reinvent an interior life where one has previously been concealed or silenced, she is speaking particularly of the "veil" dropped on black consciousness in slave narratives. One senses a synchronicity of purpose in Silko's plea that we remember "the stories, without them we are nothing," or in Anzaldua's insistence on a weave of stories rendered in cross-pollinated language, or in Norris's shimmering parables of the Plains. Even more striking, however, is the synchronicity of method: The route to reconstructed consciousness moves from meaningful image to extrapolated text and, in the process, unfolds Dillard's psychic Pittsburgh just as surely as Anzaldua's psychic Borderlands.

Notes

1 Paula Gunn Allen emphasizes the multiple roles in which Yellow Woman is cast by juxtaposing several versions of Yellow Woman stories in *Spider Woman's Granddaughters: Traditional Tales and Contemporary Writing by Native American Women* (New York, Fawcett Columbine: 1989), pp. 197– 256.

2 For a discussion of how learning alternative stories liberates one's own stories, see Victoria Ekanger's "Touchstones and Bedrocks: Learning the Stories We Need" as collected in *The Intimate Critique: Autobiographical Criticism*, Freedman, Frey, and Zauhar, eds. (Durham, Duke University Press: 1993), pp. 93–99.

◆ 4 ◆

The Caught and Connected Reader

Earlier chapters have explored some of the ways that contemporary female autobiographies can be used as valuable repositories of female development (particularly in self-definition and the forming of value systems). Many of the influential ideas emanate from the shared work of female clinicians at the Stone Center at Wellesley College and emphasize identity and value models achieved through "relational differentiation and elaborations" (rather than through the Freudian/Eriksonian models of separation and individuation). These ideas find their resonance in the personal narratives of Dillard, Simon, Gornick, Chernin, Angelou, and Walker, where the mirroring of the self in the mother, since it is never severed, forms the "precursors of women's styles of learning, of pleasure, of self-enhancement in relatedness" (Surrey, 1991, p. 57).

Psychologists Janet Surrey and Judith Jordan foreground the work of Heinz Kohut, in particular his examination of "empathy," "the reso-nance of essential human alikeness" as particularly reflective of female development (Jordan, 1991, p. 96). Women come to know themselves within relationship, what in Kohut's language is "the understanding human echo." Empathy, with its stress on flexible boundaries of a "self" and the "intersubjective" relating of people in value formation, although obviously useful as a therapeutic aid for counselors and psychologists, is also a valuable artistic lens. Trained on women's journals, it allows us to focus on the relationship of the female diarist to her material—the life she describes as she re-enacts it; to her sources of authority—the "truth value" of her self-disclosure; and to her audience—the readers with whom she is empathetically engaged and whom she empowers with her story.

If, for women, the primary experience of "self" is relational, that is, the self is organized and developed *in the context* of important relationships (Miller's "self-in-relation" theory), then women's life stories—particularly those kept by authors of public achievement who see as part of their artis-tic mandate sharing their story with a particular readership—provide keen insights on how self-inscription evolves and what it chooses to signify.

Unlike Erikson's (1963) "stages" describing male development—autonomy, self-reliance, independence, integrity, "closure of identity"—women's personal narratives describe how identity emerges when embedded within relationship. Further, by appeal and by example, they open dialogue with "resonant" readers, fostering growth and development through "a confirming and understanding human echo" (Kohut, 1978).

Journals: The Pact Between Writer and Reader

This chapter investigates the "pact" negotiated between author and reader in journals such as *Journal of a Solitude* and *At Seventy* by May Sarton, *Plaintext* and *Remembering the Bone House* by Nancy Mairs, *The Cancer Journals* by Audre Lorde, and *Daybook: The Journal of an Artist* by Anne Truitt. The particular advantage of using these texts, ones that reflect wide differences in age, class, race, health, and sexual preference, is that they qualify the notion that there exists a stable category called "women" and thus a consistent genre called "women's autobiography." Instead they illustrate the wide appeal of autobiographies and the wide range of "resonance" within readers.

Sidonie Smith and Pat Schweickart have explored the relationship forming the "pact" between the reader and the writer of autobiography. What contract is negotiated? How does gender, in particular (but also race, age, health, sexual preference) affect the reader's access to the author's experience?

Much has already been written about female modes of communication beneath the dominant (phallocentric) discourse.[1] Critics generally assume that since the male gender is encoded in the speech and signification of western culture, the language we all learn, its structure, and the ways it conveys meaning require a schizophrenic response in the female reader, one mediated by "cross-reading." As Pat Schweickart puts it in "Reading Ourselves" (1986):

> [The female reader] reads the text both as a man and a woman. But in either case, the result is the same: she confirms her position as other. Taking control of the reading experience means reading the text as it was *not* meant to be read, in fact, reading it against itself. (p. 32)

If the female reader is required to bifurcate her responses in relation to much of canonized western literature (in order to "identify" with a white male, heterosexual protagonist), how is that dynamic altered when the author's identity and value structure approximate the reader's? In short, how am "I" connected to the speaking voice within the autobiographical text and how is that voice speaking to me?

Seen in this light, it is not difficult to understand the enthusiastic reader response to Sarton's journals, with their insistence on "growing into age" and differentiating between chosen solitude or imposed loneliness; to Nancy Mairs's autobiographical essays, with their emphasis on negotiating the difficult seasons in a marriage and motherhood or combating recurrent bouts with debilitating depression and MS; to Audre Lorde's *Cancer Journals* chronicling of her "depersonalization" by the medical establishment while undergoing and recovering from a radical mastectomy; or to Anne Truitt's relational struggles with her children even as she receives acclaim as a sculptor. What is crucial to each author's development hooks an empathetic reader into a chain of "mutual empowerment."

Artists such as Sarton, Mairs, Lorde, and Truitt have used the published journal as an honest seismograph of their own feelings. In speaking in their own words about the dailiness of their own experience, their journals can correct, challenge, and—when appropriate—confirm the relational ideals postulated by developmental theorists. They can also illumine the "pact" between author and "resonant" reader.

May Sarton has acknowledged, at first grudgingly and then enthusiastically, the importance of her seven journals as one continuous means of telling the story of a human life satisfying to a huge readership. Although she insists they are not strict "autobiographies" or "memoirs," Sarton's journals constitute a form of personal narrative at once fragmentary and discontinuous enough to satisfy poststructuralist ideas about the vagaries of the "self," and powerful enough to link a reader's consciousness to the author's testimony. Each of Sarton's journals was composed on the heels of personal crisis, when self-assessment was crucial for restoring emotional balance and spiritual health. *Journal of a Solitude* (1973) marks the end of a powerful love affair; *The House by the Sea* (1977) is precipitated by the move from Nelson, New Hampshire to York, Maine; *Recovering* (1980) emerges from a year of crisis involving cancer, a broken love affair, and frustration over mixed reviews of her work in fiction and poetry; *At Seventy* (1984) records the credits and debits of old age; *After the Stroke* (1988) describes the effects of a stroke suffered shortly before her seventy-fifth birthday; *Endgame* (1992), published in her seventy-ninth year, documents illness that requires "learning to become dependent."[2]

Although rooted in idiosyncratic experience, Sarton's journals seek to connect with a wide readership by revealing the need to create order out of chaos, re-entry out of withdrawal, health out of illness. Her efforts to define "self" and "values" within a communal context, in part supplied by readers' responses, link her journals to current theory exploring women's development. *Encore: A Journal of the Eightieth Year* (1993) traces the consciousness that comes when one recognizes that time is limited.

If the story of one woman's life provides a script the reader enters, resignifies, and in some collaborative sense makes her own, then, as Carolyn Heilbrun has suggested in *Writing a Woman's Life*, artists like Sarton who speak about aging and death, about homophobia, about the narcissism of the academic and publishing worlds—who create new narrations from the raw data of life experience—free others to imagine conditions by which they may live. Age and the authority of many books, says Heilbrun, confer a "bravery and power," and writers like Sarton (and Heilbrun herself) can exercise that authority by continuing "to take risks, to make noise, to be courageous, to become unpopular" (pp. 17–18).

The process of collaboration with the reader is a gradual, cumulative one in Sarton's journals. *Journal of a Solitude* and *At Seventy*, although written 11 years apart, are triggered by similar impulses. Sarton casts herself as a character in her own story, recreating significant life experience, pondering its shape, discovering its outcome. Much like the novelist who discovers her characters beginning to exert wills of their own, Sarton sets her plot in motion, discovering its significance in the retelling. Simultaneously she deepens meaning by concentrating on a few repeating images (home, animals, significant friendships), which function as poetic metaphors shimmering with collective content. Her awareness of audience widens from the reader-over-the-shoulder peepsight of *Journal of a Solitude* to much more direct address in *At Seventy*.

Journal, spanning the year from September 1970 to September 1971, retells the story of her own artistic imprisonment figured by the claustrophobic enclosure in Nelson, New Hampshire. She begins with the need to "break through into the rough, rocky depths to the matrix itself" (p. 12). Since she declares she "can think something out only by writing it," this journal becomes an inspection, largely self-motivated, by which she hopes to understand a failed love affair, a writer's refuge that became a prison, and the serious depression that followed.

At Seventy is a direct invitation to an audience. Moved by the physical beauty of her "house by the sea" in York, Maine, Sarton captures moments, "essences" as she calls them, that link landscape with consciousness. As she explores the cycle of the seasons, the reader is invited to ponder growth and death. As she records the antics of her birds, squirrels, "wild cats," and Sheltie dog, the reader examines loyalty, dependence, and the value of trust. She struggles with the censor who sits on the shoulder of all who write with the expectation of publication, insisting that honesty is the only path to "the bedrock of truth."

> Forgiveness cannot be achieved without understanding, and understanding means painful honesty first of all, and then the ability to detach oneself and look hard without self-pity, at the cause for violent behavior. (p. 196)

Reading *Journal* and *At Seventy* together reveals a process of value formation. Each creates a context for the other, extending and deepening the meaning of Sarton's struggles with age, literary recognition, sustained love relationships. In *Women's Ways of Knowing* (1986), Belenky, Clinchy, Goldberger, and Tarule call such referential building of insight "constructed knowledge."

> Most constructivist women actively reflect on how their judgments, attitudes, and behavior coalesce into some internal experience of moral consistency. More than any other group, they are seriously preoccupied with the moral and spiritual dimension of their lives. Further, they strive to translate their moral commitments into action, both out of the conviction that "one must act" and out of a feeling of responsibility to the larger community in which they live. (p. 150)

As Sarton arrives at an insight worked and reworked through the fabric of a "reconstructed life," so does her caught and connected reader.

A revision of life is precisely what triggers *Journal of a Solitude*. It is written, Sarton suggests, in part to correct an earlier rendering of her Nelson experience in the memoir *Plant Dreaming Deep*. Published in 1968, *Plant Dreaming Deep* tells the story of a woman who, at 45, takes the risk of buying, renovating, and deciding to live alone in a house geographically and emotionally removed from friends and the artistic community of Cambridge, Massachusetts. The tale is a triumphant one, the story of a great adventure that succeeds. Missing are accounts of the destructive forces Sarton meets en route: a literary agent who fears the candor of her lesbian novel, a wrongheaded review of her selected poems, the grinding loneliness of geographic isolation, the first awareness of physical deterioration. *Journal* revises that other "script," retelling both the Nelson story and current life experience with rage, isolation, and depression factored in.

When one chooses solitude as a condition of life, "there is nothing to cushion against attacks from within, just as there is nothing to help balance at times of particular stress or depression" (*Journal*, p. 16). Keeping a daily record allows Sarton to stitch emotional fragments into a pattern, one that reduces the emotional vulnerability of the moment. *Journal* also corrects the "myth of a false Paradise" perpetrated in *Plant Dreaming Deep*. The house in Nelson that had begun as a refuge for the artist who wanted to withdraw from the clutter and demands of her life in Boston, becomes, in "revision," a trap, a place of "anguish and unrest."

Home is a metaphor in all of Sarton's writing, so her move from an inland village house in New Hampshire to a spacious rambling coastal house in Maine is crucial. "Wild Knoll" in York, with its magnificent grassy path to the sea, pulls the writer's focus outward. New geographical space has its parallel in new interior space. Solitude becomes a condition analogous to the ebbs and tides of the sea, and identity and values emerge from connection rather than withdrawal: "One does not 'find oneself' by pursuing oneself, but on the contrary by pursuing something else and learning through some discipline or routine who one is and wants to be" (*House by the Sea*, p. 180).

In York, Sarton begins the reciprocal explorations common to her next three journals but most vividly rendered in *At Seventy*: what connections and what separations are healthy for the artist to maintain; how one preserves the "primary intensity" necessary for art while still meeting obligations to friends, neighbors, and the large literary and intellectual community responding to the work; how one may maintain self-reliance and still acknowledge the fears attendant to old age, physical deterioration, and flagging energy.

In *At Seventy*, the writer's relationship to her "home" is still at the vital center, but fear is recognized, weighed, and credited with its proportional cost. And frequently the ritual of writing in the journal is a tool for recovery, providing, as it does, the discipline necessary for renewed concentration and perspective.

At Seventy balances the anxieties of old age marked by an irregular heart, a cancer scare, the death of "dearest love" Judy Matlack, with the celebrations of "growing into age" and its earned rewards: a huge and growing appreciative audience, excellent book sales, the financial security to support worthy friends and projects she believes in deeply. Here May Sarton's most vital values resonate: balance, commitment, connection. As her journal opens she assesses 70 years of life experience.

> If someone else had lived so long and could remember things sixty years ago with great clarity, she would seem very old to me. But I do not feel old at all, not as much a survivor as a person on her way. (p. 1)

Surely much of what Sarton knows about attachment comes from her relationship with Judy Matlack, a figure always a presence in *Journal of a Solitude* but fully fashioned in *At Seventy*. Judy first appears in a wheelchair, the victim of Alzheimer's disease, reduced to a baby "for whom food is the only real pleasure." Although Sarton visits her in a nursing home in Concord and bravely arranges short trips for her to York, most visits carry a high price tag.

Only after her death, when Judy "begins to live again," can Sarton remember.

> Judy is the precious only love with whom I lived for years . . . only Judy gave me a home and made me know what love can be. She was the dear companion for fifteen years, years when I was struggling as a writer. We were poor then. . . . But strangely enough I look back on those years as the happiest ones. And that is because there was a "we." (*At Seventy*, p. 217)

Although Judy is the primary example of a "we," Sarton's inventory of her life is packed with "connections." They crowd the page: friends of her youth, visiting artists, Mr. Webster who fixes the pipes, Eleanor Perkins who cleans the house, Nancy who makes order out of the chaos of the files, Sister Lucy who plows and builds at the commune H.O.M.E. in rural Orland, Maine. And in *At Seventy* Sarton clearly acknowledges the growing community of readers who buy and read her work, queue up for book signings, write literally pounds of mail monthly, and turn out in staggering numbers at her readings. This community of response leads her to write, "The answer is not detachment as I used to believe but rather to be more deeply involved—to be attached." The "self" in *At Seventy* is defined by connection to others, and values become luminous in what Saul Bellow described as "the company of others attended by love."

In *Writing a Woman's Life*, Heilbrun documents how few women of Sarton's generation acknowledged their debts to other women. She includes in this debt not only literary apprenticeships, but the forgotten or unacknowledged support of female friendship. She describes one startling exception by retelling the story of Vera Brittain's and Winifred Holtby's (schoolmates at Oxford, post-World War I) lifelong and life-giving friendship. Holtby seems to anticipate much of what gender theorists now document, and in her book, *Women and a Changing Civilization* (1935/1978), she ranges over issues everywhere apparent in Sarton's narratives.

> I think that the real object behind our demand is not to reduce all men and women to the same dull pattern. It is rather to release their richness of variety. We are still greatly ignorant of our own natures. We do not know how much of what we usually describe as "feminine characteristics" are really "masculine" and how much "masculinity" is common to both sexes. Our hazards are often wildly off the mark. We do not know—though we theorize and penalize with ferocious confidence—whether the "normal" sexual relationship is homo- or bi- or hetero-sexual. We are content to make vast generalizations which quite often fit the facts enough to be tolerable, but which—also quite often—inflict indescribable because indefinable suffering on those individuals who cannot without pain conform to our rough-and-

ready attempt to make all men [and women] good and happy. (as quoted in Heilbrun, p. 106)

Sarton's script speaks to those who "walk more delicately" among definitions. Its authority rests with those who celebrate "their richness of variety" and who may find in her texts liberating validation.

To read Sarton's *Journal of a Solitude* juxtaposed with *At Seventy* is analogous to experiencing the series of remarkable self-portraits Goya painted in his late years. The portraits move from self-enclosure, the artist locked in the self-contemplation of a window pane, mirror, or canvas, to a figure in three-quarter turn, looking outward toward audience as if to check *in their responses* the authentic outline.

Audre Lorde's *Cancer Journals*, a slim volume of 77 pages first published in 1980, offers in place of May Sarton's slowly exfoliating story, a life experience with cancer that delivers a short upper-cut to the consciousness. Lorde announces her purpose in keeping and deciding to publish the journal in the introduction.

> Each woman responds to the crisis that breast cancer brings to her life out of a whole pattern, which is the design of who she is and how her life has been lived. The weave of her everyday existence is the training ground for how she handles crisis. Some women obscure their painful feelings surrounding mastectomy with a blanket of business-as-usual, thus keeping those feelings forever under cover. For women, in a valiant effort not to be seen as merely victims, this means an insistence that no such feelings exist and that nothing much has occurred. For some women it means the warrior's painstaking examination of yet another weapon, unwanted but useful.
>
> I am a post-mastectomy woman who believes our feelings need voice in order to be recognized, respected, and of use. . . . I have tried to voice some of my feelings and thoughts about the travesty of prosthesis, the pain of amputation, the function of cancer in a profit economy, my confrontation with mortality, the strength of women loving, and the power and rewards of self-conscious living. (p. 9)

The journal entries begin about three months after her modified radical mastectomy and extend into the process of "integrating this crisis into my life" (p. 10). Lorde's journal, though nominally about cancer, the unique threat and paralyzing fear it evokes, has a second subject, a "deep subject": a challenge issued to women who choose "prosthesis in order to seem 'the same as before'" and in so doing deny the opportunity to examine the life-altering crisis. Lorde sees social conformity as the greatest victimizer of such women: social customs that urge silence in the face of loss, pain, grief; cosmetic devices to conceal cancer's amputations; conventional wisdoms that tell women to "look on the bright side" when such euphemisms are actually "used for obscuring certain realities disturbing the status quo" (p. 74).

Lorde's journal ultimately addresses what recovery is by subtracting what it is NOT. It is *not* wearing a false breast. It is *not* adopting a positive frame of mind, since negativity may be imagined to "have caused cancer in the first place." It is *not* the refusal to examine pain, mutilation, as another reality powerfully present in life. Recovery is using the cancer experience as another strategy to combat oppression—against passive victimhood, against the threat of diminished sexual attractiveness in women, against silencing, or censoring, or inhibiting honest emotions from finding their appropriate modes of expression.

The journal is composed of entries, usually short and impressionistic, that document what it feels like to be biopsied, prepared for surgery, undergoing an operation that "looks death in the face" (p. 47). Joined to these entries, often as their natural consequence, are assessments about the experience. In both types of writing Lorde speaks directly to a reader. Sometimes that reader is "generic woman," she who may, through ignorance or fear, allow cancer to go undetected. At other times Lorde speaks especially to blacks and/or lesbians, using the denials and distortions in cancer's appearance as metaphors for pervasive cultural and social oppression. This position climaxes in a scene Lorde describes where she is visited by a well-intentioned but obtuse volunteer for the Reach for Recovery program. The volunteer, herself a survivor of a radical mastectomy, shows Lorde the exercises necessary to strengthen arm and chest muscles, brings her a white lambswool prosthesis, and goes into her prepared speech about coping with the fear of diminished attractiveness.

> As a 44 year old Black Lesbian Feminist, I knew there were very few role models around for me in this situation, but my primary concerns two days after mastectomy were hardly about what man I could capture in the future. . . . My concerns were about my chances for survival, the effects of a possibly shortened life upon my work and my priorities. . . . A lifetime of loving women had taught me that when women love each other, physical change does not alter that love. It did not occur to me that anyone who really loved me would love me any less because I had one breast instead of two, although it did occur to me to wonder if they would be able to love and deal with the new me. So my concerns were quite different from those spoken to by the Reach for Recovery volunteer, but not one bit less crucial nor less poignant. (p. 56)

Ultimately, Lorde sees in the cancer experience the attempt by medical practitioners, volunteers for "Recovery," counselors, and the like, a reinforcement of "society's stereotype of women . . . our appearance is all, the sum total of self" (p. 57). The missed opportunity is the examination of one's interior life that occurs with acute physical and emotional trauma. When this is not denied, when death is permitted to exert its full claim on consciousness as a possible coequal with life, then our pact with life is altered. As women open themselves "more and more to the genuine conditions" of their lives, they grow "less and less willing to tolerate" controls over identity or values. "Once I face death as a life process, what is there possibly left for me to fear? Who can ever really have power over me again?" (p. 61).

As Lorde's insistence on examining the interior life that is revealed through suffering and authentic "recovery" links her journal to Sarton's journals, so her insistence on sharing what is private links her to Anne Truitt.

In *At Seventy* Sarton admires a journal by Anne Truitt, which the publisher has sent her in proof to review. She emphasizes a passage in Truitt describing a Rembrandt self-portrait looking steadily, "straight out" as the testimony to being "human beyond reprieve"; for, as she says, "he looks out from this position, without self-pity and without flourish, and lends me strength" (p. 50). In Anne Truitt's passage, Sarton locates an objective for herself. "It is that kind of honesty I have been after in the journals, but I envy the painter who does not have to use elusive, sometimes damaged, often ambivalent words" (p. 50).

Daybook: The Journal of an Artist, published in 1982, was written by Anne Truitt over a period of seven years. The journal is triggered by two retrospectives of her work (in sculpture and painting) in December 1973 and in April 1974: the first at the Whitney Museum of American Art in New York, the second at the Corcoran Gallery of Art in Washington.

> The force of this concentrated and unprecedented attention to my work, and to me, swept over me like a tidal wave. The objects that I had been making for years and years were drawn into visibility and, many of them for the first time, set forth to the public eye. . . . It slowly dawned on me that the more visible my work became, the less visible I grew to myself . . . my failure to come to terms with these feelings as I was making the work had deprived me of myself in these most profound depths. It was as if the artist in me had ravished the rest of me and got away scot-free. (p. 9)

The impetus for beginning her journals is Sarton-like in its insistence on examining the loss of "self" despite high artistic productivity; it is Lorde-like in its insistence on examining the interior life revealed in a moment of crisis. It stands in sharp contrast, however, in that it describes the creative process of a visual artist, which involves mental and emotional conceptualization as well as "whole body" physical execution. This is how she describes her early work in plaster.

> Plaster has such grace. Working with it is like making love. And the same with clay. The fascination of mixing clay. The wedging of earth colors, minerals, back into the earth in order to make a near earth all of your own conception, consciously brought into being. The delicate strength of tools for work in clay and plaster; the ways in which they adroitly extend the sensual ability of the hand; their actual beauty is themselves—wire bound to wood, steel toothed and curved and pimpled with rasp. My hands loved, too, the feel between them of what they had formed. . . .
>
> It was not my eyes or my mind that learned. It was my body. I fell in love with the process of art, and I've never fallen out of it. I even love the discomforts. At first my arms ached and trembled for an hour or so after carving stone; I remember sitting on the bus on the way home and feeling them shake uncontrollably. My blouse size increased by one as my shoulders broadened with muscle. My whole center of gravity changed. I learned to move from a center of strength and balance just below my navel. From this place, I could lift stones and I could touch the surface of clay as lightly as a butterfly's wing. (p. 128)

She uses the framework of her art, "a process so absorbing as to be its own reward" (p. 129) to examine the less visible contours of her own identity, a journey that takes her back to childhood and relationships with a remarkable but distant mother who died at 56 of a brain tumor, and a father who loved Anne extravagantly and also drank extravagantly, her first lesson in "loving someone you don't entirely respect."

Assessments of her parents lead to evaluations of her own role as a mother, descriptions of three children she has raised after separation and divorce from her journalist husband, James, after 22 years of marriage. She witnesses her oldest daughter, Alexandra, birthing a son and "looks back over telescoped years" knowing she cannot protect her children from the endurances and pains of their own parenthood; she cannot take "the suffering of my children on myself" (p. 173).

She tends her son through the ordeal of a serious automobile accident in which he sustains serious internal injuries and a broken pelvis. Although healing, he will "remain broken" and cannot be "fixed as I can fix some of my sculptures carelessly damaged" (p. 191). "His recovery is marked by an increasing independence for both of us, a feeling of health and ease, as if, in some mysterious way, he had accomplished his second birth, into adulthood, by means of this violent accident" (p. 192).

She speaks, too, of an evening when she in her 50s, another woman in her 40s, another in her 30s, and her teenaged daughter Mary spoke of the fears and freedoms implicit in the recognition that none (with the possible exception of Mary) would ever again wholly depend on a male for financial and emotional sustenance. Although financial insecurity and its panicky moments reappear with some frequency in *Daybook*, Truitt offers few characterizations of the reasons for her divorce. Her glimpses of her marriage and relationship with her husband are tributes: to love; to support in childless years when, after a heartbreaking series of visits to fertility specialists because of ovulation problems tied to peritonitis as a teenager, she conceived their children at the age of 34, 36, and 37; to a kind of *mutual* acceptance of a domestic life that privileged his career above hers, that required house guests and mandatory entertaining, and that left virtually all child care in her hands and the hands of a nanny she engaged three days a week to free up studio time. Truitt sees herself as an accomplice, not a victim, in a system both she and her husband accepted unquestioningly, and uses her marriage and her experience with parenthood as a means of assessing personal freedom and the life-giving independence and self-reliance withheld sometimes in the name of love. She summarizes her feelings about intimacy and autonomy in this quote from Rilke (*Letters: 1910–1926*), which she sends to her daughter, Mary, on her wedding day.

> Once the realization is accepted that even between the closest human beings infinite distances continue to exist, a wonderful living side by side can grow up, if they succeed in loving the distance between them which makes it possible for each to see the other whole against the sky. (p. 213)

Through all of her personal assessments runs the examination of the role of the artist, how her decision to pursue her art full-time made her "set sail against prevailing winds." The decision remains a mysterious one, triggered by the recognition that "I could use the energy I had been putting into endurance to *change* my life" (p. 40). She characterizes it as a "stubborn selfhood" and carefully distinguishes that plainspoken truth from the excessive romanticizing of the artist.

> The Renaissance emphasis on the individuality of the artist has been so compounded by the contemporary fascination with personalities that artists stand in danger of plucking the feathers of their own breast, licking up the drops of blood as they do so, and preening themselves on their courage. It is NOT surprising that some come to suicide, the final screw on this spiral of self-exploitation. And particularly sad because the artist's impulse is inherently generous. But what artists have to give and want to give is rarely matched and met. (p. 115)

When she feels the seductions of "preening on her own courage" she reminds herself that her personal experience, as unique and precious as it seems, "gains perspective in the total flow of humanity" (p. 224).

To see this pattern is humbling. My children's lives seem gently but inexorably to round my own as if enclosing it in a crystal ball wherein I see it entire. And see clearly what I have until now seen only darkly: that what is done is past, spun out of me in a few threads, scarcely discernible, woven into the immense generalization of human life. (p. 225)

The Reader as Target: Closing the Distance

If journals such as those of May Sarton and Audre Lorde and Anne Truitt employ strategies that make it impossible for readers to read "objectively," then Nancy Mairs forces the reader to take the next step: to use the text as a lens on one's own experience.

As Mairs suggests of personal experience, "beneath its idiosyncrasies lie vast strata of commonality, community. . . . Our stories utter one another. . . . I invite you into the house of my past, and the threshold you cross leads you into your own" (*Remembering the Bone House*, p. 11).

Nancy Mairs, the author of five collections[3] of autobiographical essays (*Plaintext*, 1986; *Remembering the Bone House*, 1989; *Carnal Acts*, 1991; and *Ordinary Time*, 1993), as well as a prize-winning collection of poems (*In All the Rooms of the Yellow House*, 1980), uses the strategy of direct assault to initially shock, then intrigue, and finally bond her reader to her text. As a twice attempted suicide, an agoraphobic, a depressive, and for the past 20 years the victim of inexorable multiple sclerosis, she possesses the heavy artillery necessary to blast a reader out of conventional expectations, polite reactions, or the avoidance of the ugly and painful. The ugly and the painful are precisely what she forces a reader to examine—both because they appear with tormenting regularity in her life and also because confrontational tactics free her from the emotional repressions she was taught to practice as a daughter, a woman, a wife, and a mother.

Remembering the Bone House is particularly clear in itemizing the damage of polite avoidance. Perhaps because it connects with a through-running narrative the crises of attempted suicides, abortive love affairs, chronic depression, and MS (she even refers to this volume as "memoir," although its divisions into segments, each with a thematic focus, are as clear as *Plaintext*'s essay format), a reader learns the high price of burying one's emotions. Emotions resurrect themselves in psychological and behavioral symptoms—ones that impede but never entirely terminate her life.

Mairs finds emotional suppression a learned response. In her family "you may prattle (indeed should prattle in order to fill silence that might otherwise turn awkward or productive) all you like, but you must not express emotionally troublesome thoughts" (p. 90). Life, even within a loving family sensitive to others' needs, becomes increasingly bottled up within emotional prohibitions.

> . . . we never confront these tensions. . . . In order to ward [confrontation] off, we have our several outbursts, get over them as best we can, and resume our routines as though nothing had happened. On the whole this process works and we all remain functional, I suppose because we persist in loving one another despite our differences. But the wounds fester. At least mine do. I can't speak for anyone else because they never told me. I wind up with emotional abscesses sealed away under scar tissue which will one day poison the lives of those in the new household I establish: the consequence of refusing permission to speak. (p. 94)

More than the family refuses Nancy Mairs permission to speak; life as a dutiful daughter, one abandoned by a father's premature death, is reinforced by an education in the 1950s that "forced compliance and docility" (p. 96). Teachers, even the best-intentioned in good Massachusetts public schools, used their authority to smooth out irregularities (which might have been creativities), to encourage "good citizenship," and to supervise even play periods into a series of appropriately gendered games (jump rope for girls, competitive marbles for boys). Outwardly compliant, Mairs is subversive inside. The battle between how she is instructed to appear and what she in fact feels, makes her an early loner, a watcher of those who seem to mesh with cultural expectations more easily. "This watchfulness [which] will grow excoriatingly keen throughout childhood, adolescence, and young adulthood . . . will turn me into a writer" (p. 45).

If writing is the strategy Nancy Mairs employs to uncover the emotional layers family and culture prohibited, her essays assault the reader with a ferocity unmatched in contemporary letters. *Plaintext* delivers each of these confrontive punches in tight, relentless, and unforgiving essays. A reader is required to stand there and take it. Absorb the punches. Look at the pain. Assess the damage. And by the by, as reader enters a pact with writer, decide which aspects of Mairs's life experience illumine her own.

Plaintext is a diet not everyone finds palatable. As one who has tried this volume in the classroom with two separate groups of gifted students and who has naively recommended it to friends and family, I have felt the force of reactions that ranged from the wary to the downright offended. To my chagrin, I could not predict who would have what reaction to Mairs. A profoundly hearing-impaired student in one class whose bravery had brought her to a western Pennsylvania college ill-equipped to handle special needs students, and whom I expected to embrace Mairs's honesty, hated the following passage:

I am a cripple. I choose this word to name me. I choose from among several possibilities, the most common of which are "handicapped" and "disabled." . . . People—crippled or not—wince at the word "cripple," as they do not at "handicapped" and "disabled." Perhaps I want them to wince. I want them to see me as a tough customer, one to whom the fates/gods/viruses have not been kind, but who can face the brutal truth of her existence squarely. . . . "cripple" seems to me a clean word, straightforward and precise. (p. 9)

A family member, herself skeptical of American culture's much ballyhooed "joys of motherhood," balked at Mairs's characterization (in "Ron Her Son") of a difficult foster child brought home from husband George's Tucson school for emotionally disturbed boys.

Lest anyone be tempted to sentimentalize the situation (and many have), to exclaim about our generosity in taking him in or his good fortune in being taken in, I must make clear that much of what followed was painful and maddening and exhausting for all of us. George and I were faced with sole and full responsibilities for a troubled fifteen-year-old in whose upbringing we had had no hand, whose values and attitudes were alien to us, whom, all in all, we could love all right but didn't much like. Anne and Matthew, then nine and five, were faced with a jealous big brother who tormented them in ways limited only by his imagination, which luckily wasn't very resourceful. And Ron was faced with an established family, whose rituals and demands were often beyond him, and whose motives for incorporating him remained obscure and baffling. (p. 45)

In addition to exploring Ron's foster care and its effects on their home, Mairs details transactions with a loathsome father who finally abandons all responsibility for Ron, the way Ron's rudimentary skills have been dulled by years of television watching, and their anxiety for the future of one "with marginal skills and even poorer initiative" (p. 51). Mairs ends the essay admitting ruefully that she probably would not "do it again, knowing what I know now . . . such ventures seem now, in the wisdom of hindsight, to demand a woman of more than my mettle" (p. 54).

In assessing why my student and my family member reacted negatively to Mairs, I discovered that what was offensive was not her brutal honesty, but rather what they felt to be the exploitation of her subject. In speaking for herself, Mairs had every right to exorcise the demons too often repressed by social conditioning, they reasoned. But in her characterizing Ron as a "dilemma," a "test case" in which the sentimentalities of foster care were forever put to rout, his personal integrity was somehow violated. He became an object—just as "crippled," her forthright "badge of courage," signified for my student a stigma she had worked for years to erase.

Mairs has found that readers who touch her incendiary essays often come away with burned hands. In the Preface to *Remembering the Bone House*, she says self-consciously:

> It is one thing to expose one's own life, taking responsibility for the shock and ridicule such an act may excite, and quite another to submit the people one loves to the same dangers. I can't resolve this dilemma to anyone's full satisfaction. But I have tried to keep my focus tight, speaking only for myself. The others all have stories of their own, some of which differ radically from mine, I'm sure. I hope that you'll remember and respect the reality of those differences. (p. xi)

Accordingly, the essays in *Remembering the Bone House* allow the reader greater distance and the context of one continuously unfolding life. While *Plaintext*'s essays, stripped of their narrative context, threaten to become polemics, manuals of instruction for those of us still ducking the big issues—disease, infidelity, social and psychological oppression—*Remembering the Bone House* throws a net over the life Mairs has lived. You may live here, too, Mairs says. If not, at least I do.

Mairs widens the applicability of her life experience by several strategies: extended metaphor, places invested with personality, and stop action photographs—freeze frames—arresting a moment of action in the narrative so that its details, closely examined, can represent the whole.

The most visible metaphor in *Remembering the Bone House* is the succession of houses that give shelter to the young Mairs and that she learns to live within. Often they are physical edifices that represent certain kinds of nurturing space: the yellow house in Maine where she remembers her mother and father's greatest happiness; the house in Exeter, New Hampshire where her adolescence and schooling took place; the cottage at Hampton Beach peopled by Garm, Pop and Granna; the farm—the wonderful retreat occupied by Aunt Jane and Uncle Kip to which she returns after the disappointments of a first year at Wheaton College and where she first begins to write. These physical places come alive not only as spaces with certain dimensions, furniture, and architecture; they also become, by a metaphoric extension reminiscent of May Sarton, the interior space vital to the growth of her individual sensibility.

> A house once loved can never be lost. Never. Sold, yes. Moved out of. But not left behind. The house builds itself somehow into your tissues. Its floor plan, the color of its walls, its smell of fir and candied orange peel at Christmas, the summer light banding the kitchen floor, the chill of September that

strokes its way up under your nightgown when you throw back the covers etch themselves into the whorls of your brain. It belongs to you in a sense no title can confer. You have metabolized it. It lives in your bones. (p. 5)

The bone house is Mairs's extension of metaphor to the body itself, its confinements, its releases, its internal dwelling. "The body itself is a dwelling place, as the Anglo-Saxons knew in naming it *banthus* (bone-house) and *lichama* (bodyhome), and the homeliness of its nature is even livelier for a woman than for a man" (p. 7). Mairs quotes Helene Cixous's words in *The Newly Born Woman* (1986), suggesting that when woman is forced to function as man's other she is alienated from herself, her body, "she has not been able to live in her 'own' house, her very body . . . they haven't gone exploring in their house. Their sex still frightens them. Their bodies, which they haven't dared enjoy, have been colonized" (p. 7).

Mairs intends to "explore her own house," for she feels that "through writing her body, woman may reclaim the deed to her dwelling." That exploration is often a painful one to read since Mairs has been plagued by a succession of physical and mental disorders that culminate in 18 months in a mental hospital: years of excruciating menstrual cramps, hemorrhaging, and migraine headaches, depression that leaves her inert for days at a time, panic attacks that make her reel with anxiety and unspecified fear. And MS appears by the time she is 30, bringing very specific fears.

It is hard to imagine, then, how Mairs's body can also be a source of pleasure. But it is. She explores her early erotic experiences with loving attentiveness and humor, just as she does not shy away from describing extramarital affairs, a single lesbian experience, and the erotic accommodations one makes to degenerative disease. That last fact of her body puts all else in perspective. She learns to remember when the body worked better, just as she learns to take the measure of pleasure by defining its edges of pain.

Memory when interrupted by tragedy and crisis has peculiar capacities to stop and start. Time, for Mairs, is often measured in quantities Before and After the onset of MS. She remembers a moment several years before the diagnosis of MS, when she felt her left foot suddenly turn under—a sign, a prediction of what was to follow; or a moment a year or so later when she first experienced the blurred vision characteristic of that disease. Sometimes an episode in *Remembering the Bone House* will start with a narrative voice that moves forward and backward in time, pivoting on the phrase, "I have three more years of good health left." These aren't, however, observations made by one in the valley of the shadow. They are not even the gaping wounds hung out on the taut line of essay to bleed, as in

Plaintext. Disease, the inexorable failure of the body, is wrapped in the gauze of narrative in *Remembering the Bone House*. As the exterior capacities of the body's dwelling deteriorate, interior space expands. For example, her relationship with her husband George, the ever patient, always accommodating husband to whom both *Plaintext* and *Remembering the Bone House* are dedicated, is caught in this freeze frame of their wedding.

> On our way up the right-hand aisle, I catch my toe in my hoop and start to trip. You can see it in the picture: both of us laughing, the bulge of my left foot behind the hem of my dress, my upper body canted forward, George's arm tensed underneath my clutching fingers to stop my fall. All the other photographs, the ceremonies and silliness of that day. This one depicts the way our lives are going to be. (p. 181)

Similarly poignant moments occur in the birth of her first child, a daughter, Anne, who arrives after protracted labor and who floods her with a love not of the sort she expected.

> I was waiting for some surge, a tidal wave of maternal adoration, the sort of suffusing emotion you see depicted on the faces of all those Renaissance madonnas painted by men like Bellini and Caravaggio. This love doesn't overwhelm me. It undermines me, gets me from below, as though I were a tree, and Anne were another tree, whose roots put out tendrils that wrap themselves around my roots, down there, out of sight. I'm suspended, sustained, in a vegetable tangle. A thicket of love. (p. 198)

And it is within this thicket that the last episodes of *Remembering the Bone House* occur, scenes that chronicle the birth of her son, her struggles with "a body in trouble," her wish to divest her husband of the sainthood she feels she's conferred on him in *Plaintext*, the public successes of her writing, and the relentless march of MS within the context of the "stubborn love of family" (p. 198). Balanced as all Mairs's texts are between pleasure and pain, she concludes:

> No end to my degeneration is in sight. I'm afraid. I'm afraid. . . . And yet . . . suddenly . . . I am washed utterly by satisfaction. Odd, that as my physical space contracts to the span of a few staggering steps, the inside of my head should grow this light and large. I am happier now, like this, than I have ever been before.
> Such episodes tend to be fragile and transient. If this sense of serenity and fulfillment vanishes, as forty-five years have taught me it is likely to do time and again, I hope I'll at least remember—while lamenting a child's long

absence, maybe, or grieving at the death of a parent, bemoaning the failure
of a book, sitting at George's deathbed, confined myself to a bed in a nursing home—that I have been, at least once, and in truth many times, happy
clear through to the bone. (p. 273)

If Mairs practices autobiographical narrative, with a vigor and drama
peculiar to her circumstances, Sarton, Truitt, and Lorde have also seen in
its capacities for metaphoric extension and vivid detail the perfect vehicle
for their observations. The autobiographical narrative becomes, in Barbara
Myerhoff and Jay Ruby's definition, a reflexive form, one with the capacity to "turn back on itself," to "refer to itself," so that "subject and object
fuse" (*A Crack in the Mirror*, 1982, p. 35). And since self-referential texts
diminish the distance between the page and the reader, they function as
instruments of discovery for the reader as well as the author.

One does not read Sarton, Lorde, Truitt, or Mairs serene in the expectation of epistemologies of growth, or tales moving to higher and higher
moral ground. Sarton's journals, for all their cumulative insights, teeter
on the edge of suppressed rage and display periods of what a therapist might
diagnose as chronic depression; Lorde's insistence on making visible what
many readers wish to avoid—the cost of being black and female and lesbian in America, as well as the costs of recovering from life-threatening
disease—forces one to examine the dead ends of racism and homophobia
as surely as the destination of recovery; Mairs's insistent, perhaps courageous, self-exposure may also eviscerate and exploit others whom she
purports to love and trust. In short, each of these life experiences offers
correctives to any notion of a uniformly calibrated or ethically superior
relational model in female development.

Artists and poets have always provided us with insurrectionist views—
glimpses into fresh ways of looking into human nature. Sarton, Lorde,
Truitt, and Mairs cast a deep vertical shaft of light on the primary personal
necessities of their lives. Each has, consciously or unconsciously, a target
reader in mind: with Sarton, often the aging woman living alone, or the
lesbian for whom militancy is not the answer; for Mairs, often the middle-
class housewife who has experienced the collapse of many of the sunnier
family values—either by attrition or the slow erosion of serious disease;
for Truitt, the woman who struggles to balance professional demands with
family alliegances; for Lorde, the "doubly disenfranchised" reader—the
black lesbian disfigured by cancer who belongs to "every minority there
is." Each uncovers in her own story the paradigm that activates and ener-
gizes her reader. Each discovers its authority, its *truth value*—what Sarton
calls "the bedrock"—*as she imparts it* to others.

Notes

1 Margot Hennessy concentrates on the reader of autobiography and within her discussion raises many questions about reader–writer pacts in the work of Smith and Schweickart. See "Listening to the Secret Mother" in *American Women's Autobiography, Fea(s)ts of Memory* (Madison, University of Wisconsin Press: 1992), pp. 295–319.

2 Sarton's latest journal, *Encore: A Journal of the Eightieth Year*, (New York, Norton: 1993), appeared almost simultaneously with a collection of Sarton's unpublished letters, journals, poems, and photographs, edited by Susan Sherman. See *May Sarton: Among the Usual Days, A Portrait*, Susan Sherman, ed., (New York, Norton: 1993).

3 Not discussed here because it was not yet available, Mairs's fifth collection of essays is called *Voice Lessons: On Becoming a (Woman) Writer* (Boston, Beacon: 1994).

◆ 5 ◆

Self-Authorization

Carolyn Heilbrun (1985) notes that "the most remarkable autobiographical accounts" of women writers have been "tucked away into other forms" (p. 14). And as the discussion in Chapter 1 makes clear, "untucking" them, coming into a voice, is a significant step in a woman's struggle to believe in the authority of her own experience, in locating herself at the heart of her discourse. The process of solidifying that authority is the focus of this chapter. Not surprisingly, self-authorization in women's autobiography occurs in a process that emerges in relation to others (family members, professional colleagues, literary models) and within the act of engaging a reader.

I see this process as unfolding in three stages, each one a prelude to the next. The first stage, represented by *Between Women* (1984), edited by Carol Ascher, Louise DeSalvo, and Sara Ruddick, describes women researching the lives of other significant female artists, a process that releases and "floods" the researcher with personal experience. The subject and researcher connect in such vital and energizing ways as to force the researcher "out of hiding" and on to the page. (This might be read as coming-to-voice, or as the completion of the "cycle" of an engaged reader.)

The second stage of self-authorization is documented by Mary Catherine Bateson's *Composing a Life* (1989), Bettina Aptheker's *Tapestries of Life* (1989), and Carolyn Heilbrun's *Writing a Woman's Life* (1989). These accounts deliberately include the author's personal life experience as part of the data base under investigation. Bateson's, Aptheker's, and Heilbrun's own life stories serve as evidence supporting and documenting their arguments. Personal autobiography *counts*, is a significant frame of life-history illustrating the thesis of the volume, these authors argue.

The third stage of self-authorization emerges from the modern African-American autobiography that employs "braiding" (of mother, daughter, grandmother stories), a blending of narratives that allows the author not only to reveal her own "text," but to claim her status as "creator of meaning" from that experience. In Carole Ione's *Pride of Family: Four Generations of American Women of Color* (1991) and Shirlee Taylor Haizlip's *The*

118

Sweeter the Juice: A Family Memoir in Black and White (1994) the authors' discoveries of self are inextricably bound within their family's heritage. It is only as we receive the *metissage*, the blended story, that we can grasp how life, self, and writing interact.

Flooding: The Power of Role Models

Between Women amply demonstrates the power one life-route can exert on another. As Jane Marcus observes in *The Private Self* (1988), "auto-biographies act as moral tales, *exempla*, like the lives of the saints to the religious, the lives of the revolutionaries to radicals" (p. 114). If one assumes that moral examples trigger not only respect but the desire to imitate, then researching the story of a powerful role model can also offer possibilities for change, for altering one's own life.

These transformations are documented in *Between Women*. In their Introduction Ascher, DeSalvo, and Ruddick describe the peculiar pleasures and peculiar difficulties that arise when one labors to retrieve, reread, and represent work on a variety of women subjects. For some, the study of women is "a pursuit of inspiration and guidance. Our contributors 'look for affinities' or 'search for authority in women.'" Others speak "of conversation . . . where the subjects act as talismans in times of change, guides and mentors. They challenge, give ideas or comfort, serving as warnings." Some contributors "are helped by their subjects," while others feel that literally or metaphorically they rescue their subjects: "They witness, nurse, . . . memorialize" (p. xxii).

> Few would even have begun their projects had they not been prompted by some as yet misty, if puzzling element of identification with their subjects. "Why so involved with a person from another century? From another race?" Identification has entailed different feelings for different contributors: strength and renewal, confusion, exhilaration, odd discomfort, pleasure, defensiveness. Studying the lives and work of women appears to offer something like the transference in psychoanalysis.
>
> . . . Clearly identification is not static: it is a process through which our essayists and their work develop. Although it may be tempting initially to fight for distance and impartiality, most contributors relax and let the stages of identification occur. It is as if they believe that "there might be a way of engaging our identification with our subjects with so little qualification or inhibition that one would emerge at the far side of the experience with a greater clarity than usually accompanies objectivity." Consequently, one way of looking at some of these essays is as a report of the process of women's identification with their subjects.

. . . Most must check their findings indirectly, through diaries, manuscripts, contemporary memoirs, as well as published works. All of our essayists are aware that, however carefully they work, their portraits are ultimately their creation—a blend of their subjects' lives and their own. (pp. xxiv–xxvi)

In including 25 essays on women subjects ranging from Ding Ling to Virginia Woolf, or Hannah Arendt to Zora Neale Hurston, and in anchoring the volume with the subjects' biographies juxtaposed with contributors' biographies, the editors of *Between Women* (who themselves contribute essays in the collection: Ascher on Simone de Beauvoir, DeSalvo and Ruddick on Woolf) point to the vital and diverse "webs of connection" that become visible when women work on women subjects.

The interactive process observable in these essays is of particular interest, mimicking as it does the psychodynamic models of daughter–mother "autonomy *and* attachment" discussed in Chapter 1. Each of the researchers also depends on a trope or extended metaphor to describe her relationship to her subject.

Of the essays, three seem particularly compelling to discuss in some depth, each sign-posting a significant interaction: Louise DeSalvo's changing relationship with the life and work of Virginia Woolf—a relationship she roots in phases of her own life, dated and fashioned as journal entries; Leah Blatt Glasser's efforts to rescue and redeem Mary Wilkins Freeman from her position of "New England Nun" to full-blown feminist; and Alice Walker's magnetic attraction to Zora Neale Hurston, intense enough to require first a mental and then a geographic pilgrimage to Florida in order to honor the writer who died in poverty and obscurity.

Louise DeSalvo begins her essay on Woolf by declaring that in her New Jersey Italian ethnic heritage women became artists in the kitchen, honing supreme skills as "fresh pasta makers." Certainly they did not excel as literary researchers. And especially not as researchers of Woolf. DeSalvo's early work on Woolf was the product of romantic infatuation with the writer.

> Early on in my work on Virginia Woolf, I thought that I would devote the rest of my life to carefully considered scholarly essays and books on every aspect of her life and art. Those were the heroine-worship days when I blanched at the sight of her manuscripts, when I did not dare to think that she had an outhouse, much less that she and Leonard used the typescripts of her novels instead of toilet tissue, that she could be hardy enough or human enough to walk across the Downs in her beloved Sussex. I saw her as an earlier generation of critics had painted her for me—frail, weak, crazy, tortured, looking out of windows, vacant, probing the inside of her troubled psyche, like the wistful adolescent on the edge of the family in the picture I have chosen for this volume. (p. 36)

She suggests that she got into Woolf scholarship "quite by accident."

> When I was in graduate school at New York University, I took a course
> with the Woolf scholar Mitchell Leaska. He was in the throes of his work on
> the *Parqiters*, his edition of the earlier draft of *The Years*. I was enthralled with
> his classes. I'll never forget the day that he brought in his transcription of
> Woolf's holograph, the handwritten draft of that novel. I changed my mind
> about what I would be doing with my scholarly life in the moments it took
> him to read to us from Woolf's earlier version of *The Years*. Here was a more
> political, less guarded Woolf. I had never known that earlier versions of lit-
> erary texts were available. It had never occurred to me before that one could
> inquire into the process of the creation of a novel and learn about the writ-
> ing process and the process of revision. It sounded like detective work. It
> was meticulous. It required stamina. Drive. It was exciting. I too would be
> working with manuscripts. I think I understood that I required a grand con-
> suming passion in a project.
>   I soon decided to work with the manuscript of *The Voyage Out*, Woolf's
> first novel, because I wanted to catch Virginia Woolf in her beginnings where
> I thought she might be least guarded. (p. 37)

As she plunges into the story of *The Voyage Out* like a crime solver stalking suspects, she discovers that she is having "enormous difficulty keeping the problems" in her own life "separate from the issues Woolf discusses
in the novel." Married and about 30 at the time, DeSalvo was undergoing
"a sexual reevaluation" and "it was simpler for me to see myself in terms
of Woolf's character than it was to look at my own problems" (p. 38).
DeSalvo gradually broke the identification she felt for Rachel, the protagonist of *The Voyage Out*, and instead of merging with her plight, tried instead
to use Rachel's life as a means of assessing her own behavior.

She worked on Woolf's compositional process on *The Voyage Out* for
seven years, piecing together its evolution from "the mountain of manuscripts, . . . letters, diaries, and journals that Woolf had written while composing the novel" (p. 39).

The task proved enormous. Among other problems, she had to separate and date earlier drafts from later drafts by scrutinizing water marks
on the paper. Once the order of the drafts was established she could begin
to correlate "the composition of the novel in conjunction with the events
that were occurring in Woolf's life" (p. 40).

> As I recorded the progress of Virginia Woolf's days to figure out what
> she was doing as she was writing *The Voyage Out*, I started realizing that this
> was one hell of a woman, filled with incredible energy, so different from my
> original impression of her. Reading about her life in London, her visits to
> the British Museum, the books she read, the jaunts down to Sussex on week-

ends, the trips to St. Ives, to Wells, to the Lizard, to Lelant, Cornwall, the walks, the work, the lived life, fruitful beyond my wildest imaginings, her engagement with the most important political and social issues of her day, her teaching of working-class people, I began to revise my picture of her and my hopes for myself. I decided that it would be foolish of me to spend endless days alone inside libraries working on Woolf when the great woman of my dreams had spent no small portion of hers walking around the countryside, cultivating important relationships, particularly with women, taking tea, learning how to bake bread, teaching, getting involved in politics, becoming an essayist, a novelist, integrating work and pleasure, and having what seemed to me, in contrast to my confined scholarly life, a hell of a good time.

That's when I bought my first pair of hiking boots and started walking, first around the lower reaches of New York State and then, at long last, through Woolf's beloved Sussex and Cornwall and later through Kent, Cumbria, Northumbria, Yorkshire. I retraced the trips she took while she was writing *The Voyage Out*; visited the places she visited; read the books she read; began having important friendships of my own with Woolf scholars; started teaching; began writing essays; started writing poetry; wrote a novel. (p. 41)

By the time she travels from Brighton to Seven Oaks to see Vita Sackville-West's ancestral home, she decides she would like to write "about their friendship, about their love affair, about their work"; tracing the evolution of one of Woolf's novels convinces her that the "creative act has been misconstrued as a solitary, solipsistic act" and is, at least in Woolf's case, more "an act nurtured by loving friendships" (p. 42). Her original posture as a problem solver sleuthing out her subject is replaced by the role of a friend, a confidante, a sharer of secrets.

DeSalvo's essay then shifts from employing the structure of the essay to the form of dated journal entries. In each she calibrates some insight from Woolf's work to an incident in her own life. Sometimes Woolf illumines DeSalvo's life; sometimes the process is reversed. Among her "life's lessons" is the example of her son, Justin, severely hearing impaired, struggling to acquire a language comprehensible to all. His struggles to move from encoded vocabulary and "a voice hardly anyone could understand" to genuine and comprehensible expression parallels her own efforts to locate and exercise an authorial voice.

Faced with misgivings about publishing her completed work on Woolf, she dives even further back into her childhood, her schooling, her undergraduate college days trying "to salvage something of myself, to try to see clearly what of my past I have tried to bury in my work" (p. 46). This journey takes her through several incidents that make her more aware of a social structure "organized to keep men dominant and women subservient" (p. 51). Woolf's life and work act as a kind of litmus paper for her own life, particularly as DeSalvo strives "to take the very best from her while managing, through the example of her life and her honesty about it, to avoid the depths of her pain" (p. 50).

> Woolf reminds us of how profoundly influential literary texts can be in the formation of character and in the formation of a nation's character.
>
> I imagine Woolf thinking, "what one must do is write a literature of one's own." (p. 50)

This is Woolf's legacy to DeSalvo "tucked away" in what began as traditional academic discourse. Engagement with Woolf provides the impetus for her own life's work, which, among other things, includes the publication of a volatile biography on Virginia Woolf (*Virginia Woolf: The Impact of Childhood Sexual Abuse on Her Life and Work*, 1989).

Leah Blatt Glasser's relationship to her subject, Mary Wilkins Freeman, is hardly one born of adoration. In her essay "'She Is the One You Call Sister': Discovering Mary Wilkins Freeman," Glasser describes the process by which her original "mission to redefine and reevaluate a New England woman who had been overlooked and misinterpreted" was altered (p. 187). Although Glasser is certain that feminist analysis will serve a writer who explores "the psychology of women's conflicts," she discovers "the process . . . is far more complex than I had imagined" and that "it involved discoveries about my subject . . . I have tried hard to evade." Not surprisingly, like DeSalvo, Glasser's work on her subject—with all its twists and turns—"became a process of self-discovery" (p. 188).

Glasser describes a process by now painfully familiar to many feminist scholars retrieving texts and searching in them for evidence of strong, independent women writing against the grain of a restrictive society. Glasser admits:

> I strategically evaded the dual nature of her work. When I had to confront the Freeman whose weaker stories were sometimes apologetic and submissive in both tone and message, I felt afraid, appalled, and defensive. Although I was dismayed by her frequent method of framing powerful psychological portraits with safe, sentimental beginnings and endings, I still tried to write out of a sense of loyalty to the Freeman I loved and selected stories to analyze accordingly. I found myself longing to rewrite beginnings and reshape endings of her stories or to manipulate details to fit my notion of a feminist model. At the time, I could not confront the complexity of Freeman's work. In my fantasy, Freeman was wholly a rebel; but in reality, like Bronte's governess Jane Eyre, she was both "rebel" and "slave," a "divided self."
>
> . . . As long as I was impelled to remake her fiction through my interpretation of her work, I avoided confronting the significant questions of why, how, and where Freeman's work became an uneven expression of self-division and conflict. It has taken me time to recognize all of this, to embark on an honest journey into Freeman's world. (p. 188)

In trying to honestly confront Freeman's "slavery" as well as her "rebellion," Glasser examines some of the buried contradictions fueling her own scholarship (the impulse to evade vs. the impulse to confront; the authority of the text vs. the need to resignify it).

> Freeman's comments on her profession inspired me because of their stress on self-discovery and self-possession. She advised young women writers to trust their own intuitions and observations of life, to be independent:
>
>> "A young writer should follow the safe course of writing only about those subjects she knows thoroughly, and concerning which she trusts her own convictions. Above all, she must write in her own way, with no dependence upon the work of another for aid and suggestion. She should make her own patterns and found her own school. . . . The keynote of the whole is, as in every undertaking in this world, faithful, hopeful and independent work."
>
> As I was just beginning to discover and define what work meant to me, I was struck by the way in which these comments showed Freeman's commitment to "independent work." (p. 190)

Freeman's commitment was won in the face of difficult social opposition. Glasser discovers, by using Freeman's letters rather than existing biographies, that she lasted "only a year at Mount Holyoke Female Seminary (1870)," that she deliberately cultivated a "love-from-afar" for a young Navy ensign, Hanson Tyler—an "unrequited love [that] became Freeman's form of self-protection, an excuse not to marry" (p. 191). In short, she created "spinsterhood" as a writer's strategy, one that permitted rebellion against her society while casting herself at one remove from that society, an "outcast," the kind of position her narrator, Jane Lennox, describes when she says, "I am a graft on the tree of human womanhood. I am a hybrid" (p. 191).

But Glasser cannot even congratulate herself on that single discovery—adjusting social disadvantage to artistic advantage—for Freeman capitulates to the pressures to marry and, at the age of 50, weds Charles Freeman for six years of dismal married life.

In having to confront Freeman's capitulations as well as her strategies and hidden energies, Glasser begins to correlate Freeman's "hybrid nature" with her own.

> In so many ways, my life had followed a pattern of complacent conventionality. Being the youngest child in the family and having parents who were already wise and accepting of adolescent behavior, I had no clear or

genuine target for rebellion. I was a "good girl" even when I wanted to be "bad." Unlike so many other feminists of my generation, I am comfortably married. Furthermore, I got married in the early 1970s when many women had decided to live alone, just as Freeman's heroines had done, but without their sexual repression. Yet somehow I managed to feel free and unexploited even within this traditional pattern. Unexpressed energies to rebel, even against my own contentment, must, however, have lurked beneath the surface. In looking back, it is not surprising to me now that I originally intended to write my dissertation on the use of the psychological double, the "madwoman in the attic" in *Jane Eyre* and in other works by women.

My need for finding rebellion in Freeman had another dimension. When I began working on Freeman, I knew that I was doing more than just discovering a woman writer of the past. I was fulfilling an established requirement that I had begun to resent—a dissertation that would earn me a Ph.D. I knew that completing the dissertation would give me the freedom to do what I love. . . . Yet I saw no connection between the act of writing a scholarly dissertation and the work I would subsequently be free to enjoy. Actively rebelling against writing the thesis could only hurt me; however, if I could find an outlet for the urge to defy the requirement by finding fictional rebellion in Freeman, then I might rebel indirectly. I confess that I still read of rebellion in fiction with great satisfaction, feeling somehow that a heroine has won me some sort of freedom by way of her aggression. (pp. 195–196)

Once she could see that she wanted Freeman to satisfy her definition of writing as a form of self-affirmation, she could drop her hidden agenda and allow Freeman's lessons to emerge as they might. She goes deeper in Freeman's stories—not simply choosing to concentrate on those she likes, but deliberately taking on those she finds boring or disconcerting. And like DeSalvo she works hard to correlate stories with Freeman's life experience at the time of their composition.

As I analyzed my difficulties with Freeman, I tried to stop thinking and writing defensively and began to think and write analytically, searching only to understand and to gain from that understanding—no more imaginary rewriting of her stories, no more remaking of her characters. (p. 203)

In exploring her own hybrid nature, her own "repressed rebel," Glasser develops a much more complicated understanding of literary heritages. And in uncovering the "real, conflicted, and struggling sister of our past," she simultaneously grasps "my own sense of womanhood" (p. 209).

Alice Walker constructs her essay "Looking for Zora" as a pilgrimage, a journey to Eatonville, Florida where Zora Neale Hurston lies in an unmarked grave. Walker visits Eatonville to reconstruct the last years of Zora's life and to mark the grave, memorializing it—wherever it may be. She describes her journey as an artistic and, in some deep sense, a personal obligation—eliciting information from a few very elderly people who knew Zora, by posing as her niece, then her illegitimate and unacknowledged niece. The "lie" falls naturally from her lips, since "Zora was an aunt to me and to all black people." Walker anchors the essay in two short paragraphs of assessment that encapsulate Zora's legacy both to her personally and to black artists everywhere.

Eatonville with its "acres of orange groves, sand, mangrove trees" is familiar to Walker "from Zora's books" (p. 432). Eatonville, an all-black town in the interior of Florida close to Winter Park, produces an old school chum of Zora—a Mrs. Moseley who, although recovering from recent surgery, agrees to talk to Walker. Talking more about herself than Zora, Mrs. Moseley provides reminiscences that nonetheless allow Walker to reconstruct much of Zora's early life and schooling via one of her contemporaries. She also comes to understand why Hurston, growing up in a "self-contained, all black community where loyalty and unity are taken for granted" (p. 436), may not have evinced much enthusiasm for integration. Mrs. Moseley is the source of some misinformation as well, and when she is queried about the circumstances of Zora's death and the specific site of her grave she replies, "She was buried down in South Florida somewhere." And "I don't think anybody really knew where she was" (p. 436).

Mrs. Sarah Peek Patterson, the director of the local mortuary, can identify Zora's burial place. She directs Walker to "the old cemetery . . . on Seventeenth Street. Just when you go in the gate there's a circle, and she's buried right in the middle of it. Hers is the only grave in that circle—because they don't bury in that cemetery anymore" (p. 437).

She is, however, more fuzzy on the circumstances of her death: "I know she didn't have any money. Folks took up a collection to bury her. . . . I believe she died of malnutrition" (p. 438).

After the shock waves of this revelation subside, Walker goes to the Seventeenth Street cemetery, plunging through weeds and high grass until she locates a "sunken rectangle that is about six feet long and about three or four feet wide" (p. 438). She settles on a gravestone and has this engraved upon it, asking the monument dealer to send her a photograph when it is completed and set in place.

Zora Neale Hurston
"A Genius of the South"
Novelist   Folklorist
Anthropologist
1901   1960

The last acquaintance Walker seeks out is Dr. Benton, "a friend of Zora's and a practicing M.D. in Fort Pierce" (p. 442). He tells her that Zora didn't get along with her family and hence when she got sick decided not "to return home." Malnutrition was *not* the cause of her death, he reports to Walker's relief; Zora was a strapping woman, almost six feet tall and "weighing about 200 pounds." Instead, a stroke caused by high blood pressure confined her to a nursing home. Her friends took up a collection to bury her, although he is also vague on the exact location of the grave.

Walker's essay ends with these two paragraphs—the eulogy she might wish to have delivered for Zora Neale Hurston.

> There are times—and finding Zora Hurston's grave was one of them—when normal responses of grief, horror, and so on do not make sense because they bear no real relation to the depth of the emotion one feels. It was impossible for me to cry when I saw the field full of weeds where Zora is. Partly this is because I have come to know Zora through her books and she was not a teary sort of person herself; but partly, too, it is because there is a point at which even grief feels absurd. And at this point, laughter gushes up to retrieve sanity.
>
> It is only later, when the pain is not so direct a threat to one's own existence, that what was learned in that moment of comical lunacy is understood. Such moments rob us of both youth and vanity. But perhaps they are also times when greater disciplines are born. (p. 447)

While she does not dwell on what Hurston's work and example have meant to her as a young black female writer from the South, it is clear that Walker envisions her own work as Hurston's enduring legacy, the "witness" of a faithful pilgrim.

Reading, assessing, reconstructing women's literary lives and work invite layered collaborations between researcher and subject, as these three essays clearly document. The assessor may find herself drowning in over-identification with her subject, drenched in empathy, as did Louise DeSalvo with Virginia Woolf. Or the assessor may find her own self standing in the way of unbiased understanding, as did Leah Blatt Glasser with Mary Wilkins Freeman. Or the assessor may feel the obligation to discharge some duty, set the record straight before her subject can be seen clearly, separated from myths or falsehoods perpetrated in the past, as Alice Walker felt with Zora Neale Hurston. The common denominators of all three narratives, however, are that the clear reciprocity between the "subject" and the "assessor" creates the real subject, and that a central metaphor ("mystery-solver," "repressed rebel," "pilgrim") serves to describe the border crossings between one point of reference and another, one angle of vision and another, one life shape and another.

Interpreting: The Truth of Personal Experience

DeSalvo's, Glasser's, and Walker's reciprocity with their subjects adds another dimension to the "truth content" accessible in women's autobiography. Such dimensions are amply documented in the work of the Personal Narratives Group at the University of Minnesota collected in *Interpreting Women's Lives* (1989). From the scholarly research undertaken by this group (composed of anthropologists, historians, literary scholars, and social scientists), this definition of autobiographical "truth(s)" emerges:

> When talking about their lives, people lie sometimes, forget a lot, exaggerate, become confused, and get things wrong. Yet they *are* revealing truths. These truths don't reveal the past "as it actually was," aspiring to a standard of objectivity. They give us instead the truths of our experiences. . . . We come to understand them only through interpretation, paying careful attention to the contexts that shape their creation and to the world views that inform them. Sometimes the truths we see in personal narratives jar us from our complacent security as interpreters "outside" the story and make us aware that our own place in the world plays a part in our interpretation and shapes the meanings we derive from them. (p. 261)

In arguing that the truths of personal narratives are subjective ones, ones derived from real positions in the world, through lived experience in relationships, in the context of "passionate beliefs and partisan stands" (p. 263), the Group honors the subjective and affirms a reader who "interprets."

Carolyn Heilbrun (*Writing a Woman's Life*, 1989), Bettina Aptheker (*Tapestries of Life*, 1989), and Mary Catherine Bateson (*Composing a Life*, 1989) claim that interpretive authority by employing their own life experience as a "test case" illustrative of the thesis they develop about women's autobiography. Their experiences, or at least the slices of experience they choose to reveal, are a crucial part of their "data base."

In *Writing a Woman's Life* Carolyn Heilbrun salutes not only the tremendous outpouring in numbers of biographies and autobiographies of women since 1970, but the new messages they report. No longer are so-called "unwomanly desires" and ambitions camouflaged, but we can read about women's ambition and anger as they move "toward public power and control." Women readers need the encouragement and example these lives supply, she argues. Heilbrun's purpose is to valorize these sorts of personal narratives and to encourage biographers and autobiographers to penetrate those forces behind the decisions and choices present in their subjects' lives and their own.

The lives of women writers are Heilbrun's text: George Sand, George Eliot, Virginia Woolf, Toni Morrison, Adrienne Rich, May Sarton, among others. She looks at the ways these writers pursued "unwomanly" ambition, dared break conventional rules, and risked more—with the result that they wrote more powerful and urgent messages. Heilbrun presses women to "share the stories of their lives and their hopes and their unacceptable fantasies," and biographers to write new interpretations of women who "have invested their lives." And in that spirit Heilbrun shares a portion of her own story. She explains the reasons why she invented her alter ego, mystery writer Amanda Cross, who, in turn, created the wry, hard-drinking detective (Kate Fansler) who, like Heilbrun herself, is a tenured professor.

Heilbrun begins her story as a super-sleuth might do, sniffing out the trail of a long undisclosed secret.

> We must recognize what the past suggests: women are well beyond youth when they begin, often unconsciously, to create another story. Not even then do they recognize it as another story. Usually they believe that the obvious reasons for what they are doing are the only ones; only in hindsight, or through a biographer's imaginative eyes, can the concealed story be surmised. I have decided, in order to illustrate the way such a story might be uncovered, to use myself as an example, analyzing the reasons why I adopted and for years kept wholly secret the pseudonym of Amanda Cross, under which, beginning in 1964, I published detective stories. Not until I had been asked repeatedly to account publicly for my decision to write detective novels under a pseudonym did I realize that the explanation I had always offered, and believed, was perhaps insufficient. (p. 109)

Heilbrun believes that women "write under an assumed name far more often than men do." She suspects that Gilbert and Gubar (1979) have identified one significant reason why: "The [women's] pseudonym began to function more prominently as a name of power, the mark of a private christening into a second self, a rebirth into linguistic primacy" (p. 110). That other naming, that creation of an alter ego that within the creator's imagination achieves "another possibility of female destiny" (p. 110) exerted real force on Heilbrun. At the time, however, she chose to see her decision as entirely practical. When she was creating Amanda Cross, who "authored" detective stories, Heilbrun herself was up for tenure. Her Columbia predecessor in the tenure process had written several novels and it was widely assumed that these counted in his rejection. "One had one's 'real' identity, and if one chose to indulge in frivolities, however skillful, one did it under another name than that reserved for proper scholarship" (p. 110).

In examining the reasons Charlotte Bronte, George Sand, and George Eliot chose "the sheltering shadow of an incognito," Heilbrun discovers some of her own: the protection of anonymity, the safety of leading an "appropriate life" while imagining a dangerous one, the desire to break through expectations and conventions with an imagined and daring life, one that "allowed the enactment of her dreams" (p. 112).

Clearly she felt the need for a "room of her own"—an impossibility while living in a crowded New York apartment with "three children under the age of eight, a large dog, a husband who had gone back for his Ph.D. in economics" (p. 112). Gradually she comes to realize that it is "psychic space" she craves, and so seeks "to create an individual whose destiny offered more possibility than I could comfortably imagine for myself" (p. 114).

> I created a fantasy. Without children, unmarried, unconstrained by the opinions of others, rich and beautiful, the newly created Kate Fansler now appears to me a figure out of never-never land. That she seems less a fantasy figure these days—when she is mainly criticized for drinking and smoking too much, and for having married—says more about the changing mores, and my talents as prophet, than about my intentions at the time. I wanted to give her everything and see what she could do with it. Of course, she set out on a quest (the male plot), she became a knight (the male role), she rescued a (male) princess. Later I found Denise Levertov's lines:
>
> > In childhood dream-play I was always
> > the knight or squire, not
> > the lady: quester, petitioner, win or lose, not
> > she who was sought.
>
> (That Kate had the help of a man is neither here nor there. We all need help. She was dependent not on any male individual but on the New York police force and the D.A.'s office, without which action was impossible.) Kate was gutsy. She also held a few opinions I now consider retrograde (such as her faith in Freud's conviction that the complaints of sexual abuse on the part of his women patients were all fantasy), but she has changed with time, she's learned, and that's all we can ask of anybody. (pp. 115–116)

Her accounts of how she chose her pseudonym are often hilarious, poking fun at academicians' attempts to plumb even the most innocent and unintentional choices for "subtexts." Amanda Cross, a name she remembers as a variant on a road sign she and her husband once saw in Nova Scotia, "MacCharles Cross," was taken to be an encoded feminist warning, "A–Man–da–Cross," by some, and a play on Agatha Christie's initials by others.

Regardless of her name, in "creating Kate Fansler and her guests, I was recreating myself" (p. 117), Heilbrun contends. And in "recreating" herself Heilbrun also begins to understand more deeply the ways in which "autobiography works in fiction, and fiction in autobiography."

> When, safely hidden behind anonymity, I invented Kate Fansler, I gave her parents, already dead, whom she could freely dislike, and create herself against, although they had been good enough to leave her with a comfortable income. (So Samuel Butler, writing *The Way of All Flesh*, recommended that all children be deserted at birth, wrapped in a generous portion of pound notes.) Carolyn Heilbrun had, in fact, great affection for her parents, great admiration for her father and a sense of affectionate protectiveness toward her mother. But they were conservative people; they could not understand her wish to remake the world and discover the possibility of different destinies for women within it. Amanda Cross could write, in the popular, unimportant form of detective fiction, the destiny she hoped for women, if not exactly, any longer, for herself: the alternate life she wished to inscribe upon the female imagination. (p. 119)

Heilbrun summarizes her relationship with the detective fiction of Amanda Cross in the past 25 years by talking about how the women's movement has affected "Carolyn's writing" ("more, more, more courageous") and "Amanda's" ("she wrote on more feminist matters," she is "an aging woman who battles despair with . . . a degree of wit and humor") (p. 120).

It is Kate Fansler, not Amanda Cross, who has become "a presence in my life," Heilbrun concludes, one who waits around corners demanding another incarnation when she's been neglected too long.

> Kate Fansler has taught me many things. About marriage, first of all. I could see no reason for her to marry: there was no question of children. But, insisting upon marrying, she taught me that a relationship has a momentum, it must change and develop, and will tend to move toward the point of greatest commitment. I don't wholly understand this, but I accept it, learning that the commitment of marriage, which I had taken for granted, had its unique force. But it is about aging that she has taught me most. She is still attractive, but no longer beautiful, and unconcerned with her looks. Her clothes she regards as a costume one dons for the role one will play in the public sphere. Her beauty was the only attribute I regretted bestowing, and age has tempered that, although, unlike her creator, she is still a fantasy figure in being eternally slim. But most important, she has become braver as she has aged, less interested in the opinions of those she does not cherish, and has come to realize that she has little to lose, little any longer to risk, that age above all, both for those with children and those without them, is the time when there is very little "they can do for you, very little reason to fear, or hide, or not attempt brave and important things." Lear said, "I will

do such things, what they are yet I know not, but they shall be the terrors of the earth." He said this in impotent rage in his old age, but Kate Fansler has taught me to say it in the bravery and power of age. (p. 120)

The anger and confrontation of early middle age, rather than the bravery and power of which Carolyn Heilbrun speaks, is the impetus for Mary Catherine Bateson's *Composing a Life*. When seen whole, this is a volume that stresses *process*, as have many of the texts in this study. Bateson sees women's lives as "jazz improvisations," "patchwork quilts," and "oriental puzzles" and she weaves together the stories of four admirable friends as if to prove these "webs of connections." Each of the four women's stories Bateson tells is intended as a "message of possibility." Her oldest messenger is Joan Erikson, who at 80 has been a dancer, writer, and jewelry-maker, happily the wife and collaborator of psychiatrist Erik Erikson. The youngest, in her later 30s, is Ellen Bassuk, a medical doctor and psychiatrist based in Boston, whose major work concentrates on the plight of the homeless. The other two are mid- to late 40s, contemporaries of Bateson herself. Alice d'Entremont is an electrical engineer turned corporate entrepreneur. Johnnetta Cole, who taught anthropology at the University of Massachusetts in the 1970s and later was an associate provost on that university's Amherst campus, is currently the first black woman president of Spelman College in Atlanta.

Bateson, whose life experience is the hub of the wheel around which the narrative revolves, has much in common with the other four. An anthropologist, now a professor of anthropology and English at George Mason University, she is also the author of *With a Daughter's Eye*, a memoir of her famous parents, Margaret Mead and Gregory Bateson.

"Each of us was once ahead of the game." Breaking into the fast line from privileged backgrounds, all five had their talents quickly recognized and rewarded. All married young, all but Alice had children, all worked hard—both within and around the system. And the system worked for them most of the time.

It is when Bateson begins her account of her abortive and humiliating experience at Amherst College in the early 1980s that the calm surface of this autobiography begins to bubble and boil. Clearly she remains unforgiving and furious with Amherst, where she served as dean of faculty under President Julian Gibbs. When Gibbs suddenly died, only 18 months after her arrival, she was first offered then denied the acting presidency. Her humiliation was compounded when she received a phone call from the new president, Peter Pouncey, asking for her resignation as dean of faculty.

Bateson's analogy—comparing Amherst with Iran in the last days of the Shah—becomes less audacious when one understands that it was the Iranian revolution that forced Bateson along with her husband, J. Barkev Kassargian, and daughter Vanni out of Iran where they were working in 1979.

> In Amherst, as in Iran, I worked for gradual change within a system that I knew was flawed, but I did not work warily enough. . . . One of the costs of living abroad, for me, was that I remained unduly optimistic about my own society . . . but Amherst was still caught in the set of inherited attitudes that defined any woman as an outsider. My optimism, which survived the Iranian revolution, was shattered by my experiences there. (p. 197)

Bateson knows the dangers of self-righteousness. "Anyone who has been involved in trying to support and encourage outsiders to move into full participation knows something about disillusionment. All too often, the noble disinherited and their advocates prove to be fractious and inept, or even vicious and corrupt" (p. 200).

Nonetheless, she finds it impossible to salvage anything but anger—white hot and perhaps purifying—from the Amherst experience. It is clear that Bateson sees her rejection as a direct consequence of two factors, both entirely ancillary to her qualifications and track record as dean: one, that she is a relative newcomer, an "outsider," and two, that she is a she.

> In any long-term community, there is a certain check on the crudest forms of self-interest because the wise know that everyone benefits from continuity and cooperation. But there is always a tendency to grab when a chance comes along—perhaps as a result of an emergency—to divide up the pie. Some people rescue survivors after a natural disaster; others turn to looting.
>
> In places like Amherst some grow to feel that the institution is their personal property, so they are more concerned with whether their writ runs than with outcomes. There was an odd mirroring between the distortions in my vision and those of a handful of senior men, equally caused by identification with the institution. I tended to identify my interest with those of the college; they identified the interests of the college with their own. The same kind of complementary distortion often happens in marriage. Women are taught to deny themselves for the sake of the marriage, men are taught that the marriage exists to support them. (p. 200)

She attempts to unravel the skein of "deception and lying" that results in her dismissal, again stressing an "all-male emergency quorum" that "ratifies the coup." The deanship is given to a member of the Committee, who fires her, an act that "bypassed affirmative-action hiring procedures for

the very person obliged to enforce them" (p. 202). Even when her tone—
often patronizing, sometimes self-pitying—undermines Bateson's legitimate anger, it is clear that she means her case to be illustrative, a representation of sexism, as it operates in the world of academic success and
economic privilege in America in the 1980s.

> Nowadays, prejudice is relative, not absolute. There is no fixed rule that
> excludes, just a different probability, a slight stacking of the cards against
> certain people, a different and more destructive standard of judgment that
> makes every effort fatal. It's like going to a gambling casino: if you know
> that all games are rigged to guarantee a certain profit to the house, you also
> know that if you play long enough you will lose everything, even if the house
> edge is only a few percent. We live in a world in which many positions are
> open to women, but there is always that slight stacking of the deck, the extra
> stress, the waiting prejudice that amplifies every problem. (pp. 204–205)

If one longs for Carolyn Heilbrun's wit and perspective in this purge,
Heilbrun would most certainly applaud the necessity for anger. Bateson,
too, sees anger's liberations.

> Anger was an achievement, a step away from the chasm of despair.
> Women in this society tend to be disproportionally damaged by such expe-
> rience, because we are too ready to accuse ourselves of failure and too re-
> luctant to surrender trust once it is granted, whether to a spouse or an insti-
> tution. Often, American men learn to project their disappointments outward,
> like Lee Iacocca using his rejection by Ford to fuel new achievements; women
> tend to internalize their losses. (pp. 205–206)

Neither does she turn on her heel and exit, teaching at Amherst another year and a half before requesting an unpaid leave of absence for a
year to think through her final decision. She decides to leave, finally, feeling
a breach of trust that simply cannot be repaired, particularly if the wrongs
are never addressed. Bateson's final words on the Amherst chapter of her
life elevate personal complaint and the need for redress to a more sweep-
ing indictment of the lack of integrity in those very institutions designed
to ensure integrity. If she is able to make her rejection instructive, this is
the warning it issues:

> Amherst is a curious place. All that confidence of virtue based on past
> donations for the training of poor youths for the ministry, now supplemented
> by tuitions in five figures to train corporate lawyers and stockbrokers. All
> those worldly and successful executives on the board, who let nostalgia for
> their undergraduate days cloud their perceptions of the present. A faculty

of high intelligence and considerable integrity cocooned in complacent myths. It is easy for an institution like Amherst College to live on its capital, but the capital that is slowly being spent is not the endowment—that continues to grow, for wealth attracts wealth—but the institution's moral capital of trust and good will and reputation.

Finally, the question is not about what was done to me or what has been done to other women. Many institutions celebrate the transition to integration by a series of human sacrifices, so that only the second or third woman in a given role has a chance of survival. After that, things slowly improve. The issue is that society supports the privileges of places like Amherst in the belief that educational institutions contribute to a consensus that involves both openness and continuity, intellectual skepticism and moral commitment. They will not do this without criticism. (p. 207)

It is this criticism that compels her book and that may signal a state of awareness where "things slowly improve."

If Heilbrun casts herself as the Fansler alter ego, the shadow to the dutiful scholar, and Bateson casts herself as the avenging angel, Bettina Aptheker sees herself as a "piecer" of quilts or a "plaiter." "Each plait is identifiable and useful in itself. Likewise, in the crossing of plaits we also see how women's experiences touch each other," she explains in *Tapestries of Life: Women's Work, Women's Consciousness, and the Meaning of Daily Experience*. Her own background defines one "plait": historian, communist, Jewish, New Yorker, a lover of Marxist texts, political theory, and, more recently, science fiction, poetry, and murder mysteries. Her story is also defined by the background and interactions with her lover, Kate Miller, a cultural anthropologist, whom she cites as a "true collaborator" on this volume. "Kate is everywhere in this book, and my references to her are simply a part of the telling" (p. 7).

The volume opens by describing a camping trip the two take together in the High Sierra mountains, a way for Aptheker to be "completely removed from academic life in the formative stages of writing." Fearful that she will simply slip into the old methodologies of her formal academic training and develop a thesis based on objective, abstract, or theoretical models, she wishes instead to design her book from the inside out—to "reframe personal experiences into women-centered perspectives."

> I am interested in questions about how to change women's consciousness of themselves, about how to help women heal from racist and sexual violence that permeates our lives, about how to restore a sense of beauty in women whose aesthetic senses are continually assaulted, mocked, and degraded. I want to explore how to promote balance in a system that institutionalizes class, racial, and gender inequities at every level. (p. 7)

Breaking the old dependencies on abstract intellectual exercise is hard, she admits; theoretical exegesis is pervasive and crippling, even—perhaps especially—in current feminist theory. She quotes Sandra Harding's criticism of current practice among feminist scholars, suggesting that in using Marxism, psychoanalysis, deconstructionism, and other theoretical frameworks they have "stretched the intended domains of these theories, reinterpreted their central claims, or borrowed their concepts and categories to make visible women's lives" (p. 10). Soon the cart begins to drive the horse and "theory," not "women's experiences," becomes the subject for analysis and research.

Aptheker's methodology wishes to shift the balance of power to the texts and away from the model used to analyze them. Looking at women's culture will be her way of "making women's consciousness visible." For she believes with cultural historian Geertz that "culture is not a power, something to which social events, behaviors, institutions, or processes can be causally attributed; it is a context, something within which they can be intelligibly—that is—thickly described" (quoted on p. 14). Her purpose, then, is "to map women's consciousness, to give examples of women's cultures, to look at women's poems, stories, paintings, gardens, quilts. . . . *From this point of view*," she argues, women's actions and values become "intelligible on their own terms." *Tapestries of Life* unfolds as a weaving together of stories, oral histories, poems, paintings of contemporary women from different races, ages, social classes, and sexual preferences, all living and creating in the United States. It is dotted with Aptheker's own personal history, her indebtedness to Adrienne Rich for "seeing the world with fresh eyes," and it is written in language accessible to scholars and lay readers alike. It constitutes women's experience, her own included, as the base of its interpretive process.

Braiding: The Personal and Cultural in One Voice

Aptheker's term "plaiting" may at least superficially resemble the process of "braiding" in African American autobiography, but I believe there is a distinct difference in how each trope functions, one that signals another stage in women's self-authorization.

As William Andrews has argued in his Introduction to *African American Autobiography* (1993), autobiography "holds a position of priority, indeed many would say preeminence, among the narrative traditions of black America" (p. 1). From the eighteenth-century slave narratives to the present, he argues, African-American autobiography has functioned on at least two levels simultaneously: first, as first-person accounts of those constrained by and yet triumphant over racism; second, as stories designed to alter the sociopolitical and cultural realities of life in America.

Andrews also emphasizes the rich opportunities that African-American autobiographies provide for the critic who wishes to deconstruct myths assuming a "universal Western standard" by which all autobiographies can be measured. If women's life writing asks questions about "selfhood" and "text," then surely the rhetorical strategies and choices for self-representation employed by black female autobiographers offer an even wider interrogation of how self (*autos*), life (*bios*), and writing (*graphs*) interact.

Francoise Lionnet's (1989) study of Zora Neale Hurston's *Dust Tracks on a Road*, one of the essays in Andrews's collection, examines one woman's literary alternative to the archetypal hero offered in Frederick Douglass's classic *Narrative*. Rather than the authorial "I" who has won his physical freedom as well as the power to write the script of his own continuing life, in Lionnet's view Hurston projects her self-revelations through the process of "braiding," weaving together identities of mother and daughter, interpenetrating the personal with the cultural, fact with myth. The result is a blended story, what Lionnet calls a *metissage* (p. 137), which becomes both uniquely personal and culturally representational. It differs from Aptheker's "plaiting," a term used, I think, to suggest the woven, cumulative strength of women's communities, in that it focuses specifically on how the autobiographer creates meaning. "Braiding" yields a truth of its own making, one authorized by the antiphonal interplay of competing voices, sifted and blended by the primary narrator.

Carole Ione in *Pride of Family* (1991) and Shirlee Taylor Haizlip in *The Sweeter the Juice* (1994) employ braiding in order to demonstrate how each has become who she is. For each, self-exploration hinges on tangled webs of ancestry and each launches out on a quest requiring archival research, travel, and even, in Haizlip's case, the hiring of a private detective. Each volume opens with an elaborate family tree. For Ione, the quest pivots on recovering information about her feminist-abolitionist great-grandmother, Frances Anne Rollin—the missing link in a genealogy of the extraordinary, accomplished women who compose her family. Rollin's diary, "tucked into" Ione's account, provides the key to "the pride of family that kept secrets and told lies—the pride that told of the men and not the women, the fair-skinned and not the dark, the privileged and not the poor—which had kept me from home" (p. 13).

Haizlip's quest is to unite her 80-year-old mother Margaret Morris Taylor with her only surviving sibling, a sister who, like Margaret, was light skinned enough to pass for white and who, with the rest of the Morris family, had disappeared 76 years ago, abandoning Margaret and cutting themselves off from "black" relatives. As Haizlip opens *The Sweeter the Juice*:

> Mysteries of color have encased my family for five generations. Putting together the bits and pieces of my past creates a quilt of melanin patches shading from dark to light, red to brown, tan to pink. There are ragged edges and missing segments. I dream I will find some of myself in those holes and gaps. (p. 14)

Ione and Haizlip reconstruct the meaning of their stories through orchestrating, harmonizing whenever possible, the interpretive voices of the past that *they* deem significant. A reader feels that their desire to ask questions is more urgent than the desire to posit "truths," and the genealogical tables that preface each volume function almost like a therapist's "genegram." The "family tree" is not simply a way of retrieving historical information; it is a means of mapping the dynamics among family members.

Ione's account depends for its impact on portraiture, a long line of extraordinary ancestors and relations lovingly rendered and equipped with recognizable voices. Primary among the dozens of voices contrapuntally woven in this story are: her grandmother, "Be-Be," a vivacious and relentlessly energetic former vaudeville dancer and later the owner of a popular Saratoga Springs restaurant; her great aunt Sistonie, "a staunch figure in Washington's black haute bourgeoise" (p. 16), one of Washington's first black female physicians; her mother Leighla, a graduate student in English at Howard University "drawn to the poetry of Byron and Milton" (p. 16), later an elegant and accomplished journalist. But even as Ione renders these remarkable women she stands at some distance from them, noting their strained interactions: the clashes of show-business, fun-loving Be-Be with Sistonie, who disapproved of alcohol, gambling, and dancing; the seemingly permanent sadness in her mother's eyes caught in the picture of her taken "around the time of her marriage. . . . I see in her face the dreams she had . . . she looks so vulnerable I cannot bear to look at it for long" (p. 16).

Distance, which confers perspective, is also achieved by the inclusion of journals and diaries embedded within chapters. Sistonie keeps two diaries, which Ione quotes from extensively. The first, *Day by Day: A Perpetual Diary*, records her travels, teaching, and health care practice between 1920 and 1929. It is a volume of rich revelations since Sistonie travels through the South in the mid-1920s as an assistant medical officer for the Children's Bureau of the U.S. Department of Labor, instructing midwives.

> As she lectured on the rudiments of cleanliness and methods of taking care of mothers and babies under less than ideal circumstances, she often found herself in towns where many blacks still lived in conditions much like those under slavery. Some had never seen a doctor, let alone a woman doctor, and sometimes she had trouble making people believe she was one. (p. 23)

She records these and other indignities, providing an eye-witness account for conditions in small southern towns in the 1920s for black females.

The second diary is a "spiritual diary dating from the late 1930's". In it she records moments of testing, the difficulties of living in accordance with her own strict moral code, and the cost of rebuffing Ku Klux Klan threats while she was teaching at Tuskegee Institute.

But it is the diary of her brilliant abolitionist great-grandmother, Frances Anne Rollin, "Frank," as everyone called her, that Ione receives and records with a kind of reverence. Initially, she treats the diary, begun in 1868, as if it may function as a kind of Rosetta Stone for her family, decoding all the mysterious hieroglyphs of the past, filling the silences, explaining the puzzles that threaten to interrupt and derail her efforts to write a seamless history.

The diary is fascinating reading and in it Ione locates the deep-seated wariness that has been her birthright. "My parents' experience had been harsher than mine, and they walked and breathed ever conscious of our color; but we had all experienced the rage of being turned away or treated badly because we were black" (p. 110). As Frank was to record it: "While the war between the sections has erased slavery from the statutes of the country, it has in no wise obliterated the inconsistent prejudice against our color" (p. 110).

While Frank's words inspire, it is not until Ione finds a leather-bound autograph album belonging to Frank in the Howard University archives that she is able to trace relationships more fully. Startlingly, on a blank page near the front of the book, Frank's lineage is traced—her marriage, her descendants—ending with "Great Grandmother/of/Carole Ione Lewis." "I was astonished," Ione says. "It was a bit like going to the moon and finding my name inscribed there on a rock" (p. 123).

That discovery, while it prompts more searches of husbands and cousins and uncles, satisfies some deep need in Ione's psyche. As her account moves cyclically to its conclusion with her caring for the redoubtable Be-Be who was her own caregiver as a child, the narrative seems less horizontal than vertical. Ione is less interested in completing the family tree with all its compelling portraiture than she is in deepening her understanding and forgiveness and compassion for the members in her immediate circle. Like Toni Morrison's felt need (in *Beloved*, 1987) to supply the interior life of slaves who had been denied a voice, so Carole Ione gives voice to the "silent" in her family and in the process supplies motives for the wariness, the anger, the strategies of self-protection, the proliferation of divorces and abandonments that have separated husband from wife, brother from sister, grandmother from mother.

Just as "Frank" Rollin's diary, precious though it may be, cannot in one supreme moment of revelation legitimate Ione's story, so the reunion of "white sister" and "black sister" in *The Sweeter the Juice* does not electrify and illumine Shirlee Taylor Haizlip's understanding of the "vagaries of race." When the two finally meet, Haizlip remembers them talking about food, the weather, cars, grandchildren. Haizlip's real subject, like Ione's, is a by-product of "the search"—the recovery of the emotional fabric of lost lives—the history of desertion, betrayal, redemption, that permits her to understand and honor those forces that shaped her and her family.

While Haizlip asserts that it is "the attempt to understand and consolidate identity that drives my exploration" (p. 15), her personal search also mirrors America's historical attitude toward skin color.

> Many Americans are not who they think they are; hundreds of thousands of white people in America are not "white." Some know it; others don't. Ten thousand people each year cross the visible and invisible color line and become "white." If a new sociological method of determining race were devised, equal numbers of black people might no longer be black. What happened in my family and many others like it calls into question the concept of color as a means of self-definition. (p. 15)

Like Carole Ione's, Haizlip's personal quest is triggered by her mother's expressions of sadness. Although married to a prominent black Baptist minister and the mother of a son and three daughters, she is a woman deprived of her past, a kind of historical *persona non grata*, the possessor of only one childhood picture and no letters, possessions, or memories with which to retrieve a sense of the past.

The need to recover a past is, of course, far wider than the need to alleviate some of her mother's pain. "My mother's story mirrors the lives of tens of thousands of Americans who have racial schisms in their own families," Haizlip adds, and part of the impetus to search out her mother's "lost family" comes from this wider need to know "what has shaped us."

Haizlip's descriptions of family are multifold and simultaneously told. On one level, she researches her mother's "lost family," tracing the fair-skinned Morris through an Irish immigrant and a mulatto slave. Margaret Maher, the immigrant who lost her mother to squalid conditions on the transatlantic journey to America in the early 1860s, was left by her father in Washington's St. Vincent Orphanage—setting the "pattern of abandonment" for the Morris side of the family tree. She married Edward Everett Morris, a former slave, and by the definitions of the day, a "quadroon." Although he looked white, he made no effort to hide the fact that he was part black and had escaped from slavery. Ruminating on Margaret's motives, Haizlip observes: "In many ways, Margaret Maher's circumstances were similar to Edward's. For twelve years she . . . had lived in a rigidly controlled, unadorned environment where all her activity was monitored . . . she too had been an enslaved person" (p. 50).

Simultaneously with this unrolling of six generations of research, she describes her father's ancestry. The Taylors are as dark as the Morrises are light, as anchored in family as the Morrises are cut adrift by abandonment and betrayal, as much conduits of family news as the Morrises are devoid of faces and feelings, letters or phone calls. Family pride allows the Taylors to trace roots to American Indian and West African peoples.

A third layer of description runs concomitant with Haizlip's tellings of her mother's and father's stories: the history of race and racism in America. For example, she begins her research on the infamous day Rodney King is brutally beaten in Los Angeles, and ends it on the day the verdict is delivered in the second King trial. And throughout the tracing of family lifelines she weaves a record of the Reconstruction, the Nat Turner Rebellion, the enactment of Jim Crow laws, segregated and integrated schools, Negro Colleges, the Scottsboro Boys, Emmett Till. The three story strands are so tightly woven as to be inextricable from one another, each shaping, defining, and pressuring the others.

Shirlee Haizlip's own story shoots out of the center of this pressure: her education at Wellesley; her marriage to Harold Haizlip, an Amherst College graduate who is dark enough to be arrested by a New Haven policeman as he drives his fiancee Shirlee, "almost white," to choose their wedding rings; her role as a mother; her career advancements as director of the National Center for Film & Video Preservation and head of her own public relations firm. Yet the fullness of her story never nullifies her desire to track down the one living "Morris relative," Grace—who is found by a detective agency—living quite close to the Haizlip family in California. She is 88 and in Anaheim. "How appropriate . . . that she should be located near Disneyland, the world of make believe" (p. 242).

Haizlip visits Grace on several occasions, preparing the ground for the hoped-for reunion between sisters. And they do in fact meet, exchange photos and gifts, promise to keep in touch with one another. Rancor is noticeably absent in their confrontation. Grace has almost "no colored memories," and Margaret comes to understand that Grace was "just a little girl" when the abandonment took place and thereafter probably motivated, especially as she came to adulthood in Depression years, by the wider economic opportunities available to one able to "pass." Although everyone seems relieved that the reunion has occurred, the long-anticipated, face-to-face meeting cannot confer authority on this story any more than the recovery of Rollin's diary could legitimate Ione's story.

That authority is created by braiding, in *The Sweeter the Juice*, the allegorical strata of racial history and a double family lineage; in *Pride of Family* by the interweaving of women's voices speaking out of diaries, photographs, and personal encounters. In both volumes, the process of grounding the personal in the historical and social circumstances common to other black lives activates a unique and individual voice.

Carolyn Heilbrun crystallizes the liberations available when female authors of public achievement see, as a part of their artistic mandate, the value of sharing their stories with a particular readership. "Women have lived with too much closure," she argues in *Writing a Woman's Life* (p. 130), and "when the hope for closure is abandoned" the seduction and ultimate imprisonment of a passive, or silenced, or deferred life are left behind. As women uncover the authority of their own life experiences, they engage in crucial conversions that confer bravery and power. As Sheila Rowbotham (1973) writes, we can "only hear silence in the moment in which it is breaking" (p. 29).

◆ Conclusion ◆

"The Finger Pointing at the Moon Is Not the Moon"

As Margo Culley (1992, p. 3) observes, "it would be hard to point to a field of contemporary literary studies more vibrant than autobiography studies." And certainly the body of theoretical and critical discourse surrounding women's autobiographies, although scarcely a dozen years old, grows at a staggering rate.

I locate special value in the texts discussed in this volume, examples of late-twentieth-century literary autobiography infused with metaphor and conscious of the shaping power of memory, because they mediate some of the debates currently raging in theory and allow us to reclaim the pleasure of finding ourselves in a wide variety of stories.

Barbara Christian, in her provocative essay "The Race for Theory" (1988), cites what she sees as a persistent danger in new academic fields ripe with theoretical controversies: that is, the "takeover" of literature by what she terms "the race for theory." "Critics are no longer concerned with literature, but with other critics' texts"; their self-referentiality with "its emphasis on quoting its prophets, its linguistic jargon, its tendency toward 'biblical exegesis'" deflects interest away from the work, substituting critical discourse in its place. "As the Buddhists would say, the finger pointing at the moon is not the moon" (pp. 68–69).

Appropriating the methods of creative writers, tracing the exfoliating patterns of metaphor and memory, for example, is one way of avoiding the "academic hegemony" Christian cautions against. Audre Lorde identifies the value of this process in "Poetry Is Not a Luxury" (in *Sister Outsider*, 1984) when she says:

> We can train ourselves to respect our feelings and to transpose them into a language so they can be shared. And where that language does not yet exist, it is our poetry which helps to fashion it. Poetry is not only dream and vision; it is the skeleton architecture of our lives. It lays the foundations for a future of change, a bridge across our fears of what has never been before. (p. 37)

The "skeleton architecture of our lives" adds to our knowledge of female development, particularly in the mirroring of the mother and the role of nurturance as it is played out in women's lives; it furthers our understanding of the pact between author and reader, of the interactive agency of the reader, and, through the universalizing power of metaphor, it seeks ways to reconcile differences within identity. But most of all it provides the necessary nourishment for writers and readers who, in the process of writing and reading autobiographical texts, come to understand their own lives better.

As much as women especially need to locate autobiographical voices consonant with their own, we do not need exact replications of our experience in order to engage a text fully. Instead, as the autobiographer "reads" her life, her reader also "rereads" her own life by association. The process of writing autobiography, reading it (and perhaps even writing about it) is self-reflexive, unified in impulse if diverse in application.

Autobiography with its border crossings—personal, narrative, interactive, associative, relational—encourages a larger view of human discourse than the "thesis-support" models dominating Christian's lamentable race for theory. Its effects are already visible in academic discourse of the sort available in *The Intimate Critique*, where the contributors were encouraged to "write the essay about the literature you love in the way you would write it if you were not worrying about publishing it in a mainstream academic journal" (p. 3). Such explorations, what Diane Freedman and coauthors (1993) call the "new subjectivity," offer alternatives to the restrictions of the "adversarial method," that is, the necessity to establish authority by destroying the competition. They also reveal why it is difficult for women, blacks, gays, Third World scholars, all such newcomers to the club, to risk the "open-ended, generative, and process oriented." Reading and writing about alternative lives, reading and writing our own lives, may provide a different venue, "a safehouse" in Audre Lorde's phrase, where we can register the stories necessary to live by.

◆ Bibliography ◆

Allen, Paula Gunn. *The Sacred Hoop: Recovering the Feminine in American Indian Traditions*. Boston: Beacon Press, 1987.

———. *Spider Woman's Granddaughters: Traditional Tales and Contemporary Writing by Native American Women*. New York: Fawcett Columbine, 1989.

Alvarez, A. *The Savage God: A Study of Suicide*. New York: Bantam, 1973.

Ames, Lois. "Notes Toward a Biography." In *The Art of Sylvia Plath*, Charles Newman, ed. Bloomington: Indiana University Press, 1970, pp. 155–174.

Andrews, William, ed. *To Tell a Free Story: The First One Hundred Years of Afro-American Autobiography*. Urbana: Illinois University Press, 1986.

———. *African American Autobiography*. Englewood Cliffs, NJ: Prentice-Hall, 1993.

Angelou, Maya. *I Know Why the Caged Bird Sings*. New York: Random House, 1969.

Anzaldua, Gloria. *Borderlands/La Frontera: The New Mestiza*. San Francisco: Aunt Lute Books, 1987.

———. *Making Face, Making Soul, Haciendo Caras: Creative and Critical Perspectives by Feminists of Color*. San Francisco: Aunt Lute Books, 1990.

Aptheker, Bettina. *Tapestries of Life: Women's Work, Women's Consciousness, and the Meaning of Daily Experience*. Amherst: University of Massachusetts Press, 1989.

Ascher, Carol, Louise DeSalvo, and Sara Ruddick, eds. *Between Women*. Boston: Beacon Press, 1984.

Atwood, Margaret. "Haunted Joy Their Nightmares." Rev. of *Beloved*, by Toni Morrison. *New York Times Book Review* September 13, 1987: 47.

———. "Monument to a Dead Self." Rev. of Anne Sexton: *A Self-Portrait in Letters*, Linda Gray Sexton and Lois Ames, eds. *New York Times Book Review* no. 6, vol. II, 1977: 15.

Axelrod, Stephen Gould. *Sylvia Plath: The Wound and the Cure of Words*. Baltimore: Johns Hopkins University Press, 1990.

Bataille, Gretchen, and Kathleen M. Sands. *American Indian Women Telling Their Lives*. Lincoln: University of Nebraska Press, 1984.

Bateson, Mary Catherine. *Composing a Life*. New York: Atlantic Monthly Press, 1989.

———. *Peripheral Visions: Learning Along the Way*. New York: HarperCollins, 1994.

Belenky, Mary, Blythe Clinchy, Nancy Goldberger, and Jill Tarule, eds. *Women's Ways of Knowing: The Development of Self, Voice, and Mind*. New York: Basic Books, 1986.

Benstock, Shari, ed. *The Private Self: Theory and Practice of Women's Autobiographical Writings*. Chapel Hill: University of North Carolina Press, 1988.

Braham, Jeanne. "Seeing With Fresh Eyes: A Study of May Sarton's Journals." In *That Great Sanity: Critical Essays on May Sarton*, Susan Swartzlander and Marilyn Mumford, eds. Ann Arbor: University of Michigan Press, 1992, pp. 153–167.

———. "'Passionate Inwardness', The Spiritual Journeys of Kathleen Norris, Nancy Mairs, and Patricia Hampl." *The Georgia Review* 48.1 (Spring 1994): 188–194.

———. "A Lens of Empathy: A Comparison of the Journals of Sarton, Mairs, and Lorde." In *Inscribing The Daily*, Suzanne Bunkers and Cynthia Huff, eds. Amherst: University of Massachusetts Press (forthcoming).

Brodzki, Bella, and Celeste Schenck, eds. *Life/Lines: Theorizing Women's Autobiography*. Ithaca: Cornell University Press, 1988.

Bruss, Elizabeth. *Autobiographical Acts: The Changing Situation of a Literary Genre*. Baltimore: Johns Hopkins University Press, 1976.

Bunkers, Suzanne. *The Diary of Caroline Seabury*. Madison: University of Wisconsin Press, 1991.

———. *'All Will Yet Be Well': The Diary of Sarah Gillespie Huftalen 1873–1952*. Iowa City: University of Iowa Press, 1993.

———. "What Do Women Really Mean? Thoughts on Women's Diaries and Lives." In *The Intimate Critique: Autobiographical Literary Criticism*, Diane P. Freedman, Olivia Frey, and Frances Murphy Zauhar, eds. Durham: Duke University Press, 1993, pp. 207–221.

Butterfield, Stephen. *Black Autobiography in America*. Amherst: University of Massachusetts Press, 1974.

Cary, Lorene. *Black Ice*. New York: Vintage Books, 1991.

Chernin, Kim. *In My Mother's House: A Daughter's Story*. New York: Harper & Row, 1983.

Chevigny, Bell Gale. "Daughters Writing." In *Between Women*, Carol Asher, Louise DeSalvo, and Sara Ruddick, eds. Boston: Beacon Press, 1984, pp. 357–381.

Chodorow, Nancy. *Feminism and Psychoanalytic Theory*. New Haven: Yale University Press, 1989.

———. *The Reproduction of Mothering*. Berkeley: University of California Press, 1978.

Christian, Barbara. "The Race for Theory." *Feminist Studies* 14.1 (Spring 1988) 67–79.

Cixous, Helene. "Stories: Out and Out: Attack/Ways Out/Forays." In *The Newly Born Woman*, trans. Betsy Wing. Minneapolis: University of Minnesota Press, 1986, pp. 63–132.

Clayton, John. *Gestures of Healing: Anxiety and the Modern Novel*. Amherst: University of Massachusetts Press, 1991.

Cooper, Jane, ed. *Reading Adrienne Rich: Reviews and Re-Visions, 1951–1981*. Ann Arbor: University of Michigan Press, 1984.

Couser, G. Thomas. *American Autobiography: The Prophetic Mode*. Amherst: University of Massachusetts Press, 1979.

Culley, Margo, ed. *A Day at a Time: The Diary Literature of American Women from 1764 to the Present*. New York: Feminist Press at the City University of New York, 1985.

———, ed. *American Women's Autobiography: Fea(s)ts of Memory*. Madison: University of Wisconsin Press, 1992.

de Man, Paul. "Autobiography as De-facement." *Modern Language Notes* 94 (1979): 920–930.

DeSalvo, Louise. "A Portrait of the Puttana as a Middle-Aged Woolf Scholar." In *Between Women*, Carol Asher, Louise DeSalvo, and Sara Ruddick, eds. Boston: Beacon Press, 1984, pp. 35–55.

———. *Virginia Woolf: The Impact of Childhood Sexual Abuse on Her Life and Work*. Boston: Beacon Press, 1989.

Didion, Joan. "Salvador." In *The Dolphin Reader*, Douglas Hunt, ed. Boston: Houghton Mifflin, 1987, pp. 630–637.

Dillard, Annie. *An American Childhood*. New York: Harper & Row, 1987.

———. "To Fashion a Text." In *Inventing the Truth: The Art and Craft of Memoir*. William Zinsser, ed. Boston: Houghton Mifflin, 1987, pp. 53–76.

———. "Total Eclipse." In *On Nature*, Daniel Halpern, ed. San Francisco: North Point Press, 1987, pp. 160–172.

Dinnerstein, Dorothy. *The Mermaid and the Minotaur*. New York: Harper & Row, 1976.

DuPlessis, Rachel B. *Writing Beyond the Ending: Narrative Strategies of Twentieth Century Women Writers*. Bloomington: Indiana University Press, 1985.

Eakin, Paul John. *Fictions in Autobiography: Studies in the Art of Self-Invention*. Princeton: Princeton University Press, 1985.

Erikson, Erik. *Childhood and Society*. New York: W.W. Norton, 1963.

———. *Identity, Youth and Crisis*. New York: W.W. Norton, 1968.

Flax, Jane. *Thinking Fragments: Psychoanalysis, Feminism, and Post-Modernism in the Contemporary West*. Berkeley: University of California Press, 1990.

Forche, Carolyn. "The Colonel." In *The Country Between Us*. New York: Harper & Row, 1981, p. 16.

Fox-Genovese, Elizabeth. "To Write Myself: The Autobiographies of Afro-American Women." In *Feminist Issues in Literary Scholarship*, Shari Benstock, ed. Bloomington: Indiana University Press, 1987.

Freedman, Diane P., Olivia Frey, and Frances Murphy Zauhar, eds. *The Intimate Critique: Autobiographical Literary Criticism*. Durham: Duke University Press, 1993.

Friedman, Susan Stanford. "Women's Autobiographical Selves." In *The Private Self: Theory and Practice of Women's Autobiographical Writings*, Shari Benstock, ed. Chapel Hill: University of North Carolina Press, 1988, pp. 34–63.

Gilbert, Sandra, and Susan Gubar. *The Madwoman in the Attic*. New Haven: Yale University Press, 1979.

Gornick, Vivian. *Fierce Attachments*. New York: Simon & Schuster, 1987.

Glasser, Leah Blatt. "'She is the One You Call Sister': Discovering Mary Wilkins Freeman." In *Between Women*, Carol Ascher, Louise DeSalvo, and Sara Ruddick, eds. Boston: Beacon Press, 1984, pp. 187–213.

Greenberg, Jay R., and Stephen A. Mitchell. *Object Relations in Psychoanalytic Theory*. Cambridge: Harvard University Press, 1983.

Haizlip, Shirlee Taylor. *The Sweeter the Juice: A Family Memoir in Black and White*. New York: Simon & Schuster, 1994.

Hampl, Patricia. *A Romantic Education*. Boston: Houghton Mifflin, 1981.

———. "Memory and Imagination." In *The Dolphin Reader: Shorter Edition*, Douglas Hunt, ed. Boston: Houghton Mifflin, 1987, pp. 695–706.

———. "The Need to Say It." In *The Writer on Her Work*, vol. II, Janet Sternberg, ed. New York: W.W. Norton, 1991, pp. 21–31.

Heilbrun, Carolyn. "Women's Autobiographical Writings: New Forms." In *Prose Studies* 8 (September 1985): pp. 14–28.

———. *Writing a Woman's Life*. New York: W.W. Norton, 1989.

Hellman, Lillian. *An Unfinished Woman*. Boston: Little, Brown, 1969.

———. *Pentimento*: A Book of Portraits. Boston: Little, Brown & Company, 1973.

———. *Scoundrel Time*. Boston: Little, Brown & Company, 1976.

Holtby, Winifred. *Women and a Changing Civilization*. New York: Longmans, Green, 1935. Reprinted Chicago: Cassandra Edition, Academy Press, 1978.

Hughes, Ted, and Frances McCullough, eds. *Journals of Sylvia Plath*. New York: Doubleday, 1983.

Hunter-Gault, Charlayne. *In My Place*. New York: Vintage, 1992.

Hurston, Zora Neale. *Mules and Men*. Bloomington: University of Indiana Press, 1935/1978.

Ione, Carole. *Pride of Family: Four Generations of American Women of Color*. New York: Avon Books, 1991.

Jay, Paul. *Being in the Text: Self-Representation from Wordsworth to Roland Barthes*. Ithaca: Cornell University Press, 1984.

Jeffrey, Julie Roy. *Frontier Women: The Trans-Mississippi West, 1840–1880*. New York: Hill and Wang, 1979.

Jelinek, Estelle. *The Tradition of Women's Autobiography: From Antiquity to the Present*. Boston: G.K. Hall/Twayne, 1986.

Jordan, Judith et al., eds. *Women's Growth in Connection: Writings from the Stone Center*. New York: Guilford Press, 1991.

Juhasz, Suzanne. "Towards a Theory of Form in Feminist Autobiography." In *Women's Autobiography*, Estelle Jelinek, ed. Bloomington: Indiana University Press, 1980.

Kingston, Maxine Hong. *The Woman Warrior: Memoirs of a Girlhood Among Ghosts*. New York: Alfred A. Knopf, 1976.

Kizer, Carolyn. "Pro Femina." From *Knock Upon Silence*. New York: Doubleday, 1965/1966.

Kohut, Heinz. *The Analysis of the Self*. New York: International Universities Press, 1971.

———. *The Restoration of the Self*. New York: International Universities Press, 1972.

———. "Beyond the Bounds of the Basic Rule: Some Recent Contributions to Applied Psychoanalysis." In *The Search for the Self*, vol. 1, P. Ornstein, ed. New York: International Universities Press, 1978.

Kumin, Maxine. *The Retrieval System*. New York: Penguin Books, 1978.

———. *To Make a Prairie: Essays on Poets, Poetry, and Country Living*. Ann Arbor: University of Michigan Press, 1979.

———. *In Deep: Country Essays*. New York: Viking, 1987.

———. "How It Was: Maxine Kumin on Anne Sexton." In *Sexton: Selected Criti-*

cism, Diana Hume George, ed. Urbana: University of Illinois Press, 1988, pp. 210–217.

Lifshin, Lyn. *Ariadne's Thread: A Collection of Contemporary Women's Journals.* New York: Harper & Row, 1982.

Lionnet, Francoise. *Autobiographical Voices: Race, Gender, Self Portraiture.* Ithaca: Cornell University Press, 1989.

Lorde, Audre. *The Cancer Journals.* San Francisco: Spinsters/Aunt Lute, 1980.

———. "Poetry Is Not a Luxury." From *Sister Outsider.* Trumansburg, New York: Crossing Press, 1984.

Mairs, Nancy. *Plaintext.* New York: Harper & Row, 1986.

———. *Remembering the Bone House.* New York: Harper & Row, 1989.

———. *Voice Lessons: On Becoming a (Woman) Writer.* Boston: Beacon, 1994.

Malcolm, Janet. *The Silent Woman: Sylvia Plath and Ted Huges.* New York: Alfred A. Knopf, 1994.

Marcus, Jane. "Invisible Mending." In *Between Women*, Carol Ascher, Louise DeSalvo, and Sara Ruddick, eds. Boston: Beacon Press, 1984, pp. 381–397.

———. "The Private Selves of Public Women." In *The Private Self: Theory and Practice of Women's Autobiographical Writings*, Shari Benstock, ed. Chapel Hill: University of North Carolina Press, 1988, pp. 114–146.

McCarthy, Mary. *Memories of a Catholic Girlhood.* New York: Harcourt Brace Jovanovich, 1957.

McKay, Nellie Y. "Race, Gender, and Cultural Context in Zora Neale Hurston's *Dust Tracks on a Road.*" In *Life/Lines: Theorizing Women's Autobiography*, Brodzki and Schenck, eds. Ithaca: Cornell University Press, 1988, pp. 175–188.

Merwin, Dido. "Vessel of Wrath: A Memoir of Sylvia Plath." Appendix to *Bitter Fame: A Life of Sylvia Plath* by Anne Stevenson. Boston: Houghton Mifflin, 1989.

Metz, Christian. *The Imaginary Signifier: Psychoanalysis and the Cinema.* Bloomington: Indiana University Press, 1982.

Middlebrook, Diane Wood. "'I Tapped My Own Head': The Apprenticeship of Anne Sexton." In *Coming to Light: American Women Poets in the Twentieth Century*, Diane Wood Middlebrook and Marilyn Yalom, eds. Ann Arbor: University of Michigan Press, 1985, pp. 195–203.

———. *Anne Sexton: A Biography.* Boston: Houghton Mifflin, 1991.

Michaels, I. Lloyd. "The Thin Blue Line and the Limits of Documentary," from a manuscript in progress.

Miller, Jean Baker. *Toward a New Psychology of Women*, 2nd ed. Boston: Beacon Press, 1986.

———. "The Development of Women's Sense of Self." In *Women's Growth in Connection: Writings from the Stone Center*, Judith Jordan et al., eds. New York: Guilford Press, 1991, pp. 11–26.

Morrison, Toni. "The Site of Memory." In *Inventing the Truth: The Art and Craft of Memoir*, William Zinsser, ed. Boston: Houghton Mifflin, 1987, pp. 101–124.

———. *Beloved: A Novel.* New York: Alfred A. Knopf, 1987.

Myerhoff, Barbara, and Jay Ruby. "Introduction: Reflexivity and Its Relatives." In *A Crack in the Mirror: Reflexive Perspectives in Anthropology.* Philadelphia: University of Pennsylvania Press, 1982.

Nicholson, Linda, and Nancy Fraser. "Social Criticism Without Philosophy: An Encounter Between Feminism and Postmodernism." In *Postmodernism/ Feminism*, Linda Nicholson, ed. London: Routledge, 1990, pp. 19–38.

Norris, Kathleen. *Dakota: A Spiritual Geography*. New York: Tichnor & Fields, 1993.

Olney, James. *Metaphors of Self: The Meaning of Autobiography*. Princeton: Princeton University Press, 1972.

———, ed. *Autobiography: Essays Theoretical and Critical*. Princeton: Princeton University Press, 1980.

Olsen, Tillie. *Silences*. New York: Delta, 1978.

Ostriker, Alicia. *Writing Like a Woman*. Ann Arbor: University of Michigan Press, 1983.

———. "Anne Sexton and the Seduction of an Audience." In *Sexton: Selected Criticism*, Diana Hume George, ed. Urbana: University of Illinois Press, 1988, pp. 14–27.

———. *Stealing the Language: The Emergence of Women's Poetry in America*. Boston: Beacon Press, 1986.

Pascal, Roy. *Design and Truth in Autobiography*. Cambridge, MA: Harvard University Press, 1960.

Personal Narratives Group, eds. *Interpreting Women's Lives: Feminist Theory and Personal Narratives*. Bloomington: Indiana University Press, 1989.

Plath, Aurelia, ed. *Letters Home: Correspondence 1950–1963*. New York: Harper & Row, 1975.

Raymond, Janice G. *A Passion for Friends: Toward a Philosophy of Female Affection*. Boston: Beacon Press, 1986.

Rebolledo, Tey Diana. "The Politics of Poetics: Or, What Am I, A Critic, Doing in This Text Anyhow?" In *Making Face, Making Soul, Haciendo Caras: Creative and Critical Perspectives by Feminists of Color*. Gloria Anzaldua, ed. San Francisco: Aunt Lute Books, 1990, pp. 346–356.

Rich, Adrienne. *Diving Into the Wreck: Poems 1971–1972*. New York: W.W. Norton, 1973.

———. *Of Woman Born: Motherhood as Experience and Institution*. New York: W.W. Norton, 1976.

———. *On Lies, Secrets and Silence*. New York: W.W. Norton, 1979.

———. *The Fact of a Doorframe: Poems Selected and New 1950–1984*. New York: W.W. Norton, 1984.

Rowbotham, Sheila. *Woman's Consciousness, Man's World*. Middlesex: Penguin Books, 1973.

Sands, Kathleen Mullen. "Indian Women's Personal Narratives: Voices Past and Present." In *American Women's Autobiography: Fea(s)ts of Memory*, Margo Culley, ed. Madison: University of Wisconsin Press, 1992.

Sarton, May. *I Knew a Phoenix*. New York: W.W. Norton, 1959.

———. *Plant Dreaming Deep*. New York: W.W. Norton, 1968.

———. *Journal of a Solitude*. New York: W.W. Norton, 1973.

———. *A World of Light*. New York: W.W. Norton, 1977.

———. *The House by the Sea*. New York: W.W. Norton, 1977.

———. *Recovering: A Journal*. New York: W.W. Norton, 1980.

———. *At Seventy: A Journal*. New York: W.W. Norton, 1984.

———. *Endgame: Journal of the Seventy Ninth Year*. New York: W.W. Norton, 1992.

———. *Encore: A Journal of the Eightieth Year*. New York: W.W. Norton, 1993.

Schweickart, Patrocinio P. "Reading Ourselves: Toward a Feminist Theory of Reading." In *Gender and Reading*, Elizabeth Flynn and Pat Schweickart, eds. Baltimore: Johns Hopkins University Press, 1986, pp. 31–62.

Scott, Kesho Yvonne. *The Habit of Surviving*. New York: Ballantine Books, 1991.

Settle, Mary Lee. "London—1944." In *The Best American Essays: 1988*, Robert Atwan, ed. New York: Tichnor & Fields, 1988, pp. 1–17.

Sexton, Anne. "The Barfly Ought to Sing." In *The Art of Sylvia Plath*, Charles Newman, ed. Bloomington: University of Indiana Press, 1970, pp. 174–182.

Sexton, Linda Gray, and Lois Ames, eds. *Anne Sexton: A Self-Portrait in Letters*. Boston: Houghton Mifflin, 1977.

Sherman, Susan, ed. *May Sarton: Among the Usual Days, A Portrait*. New York: W.W. Norton, 1993.

Showalter, Elaine. "Feminist Criticism in the Wilderness." In *Writing and Sexual Difference*, Elizabeth Abel, ed. Chicago: University of Chicago Press, 1982, pp. 9–36.

Silko, Leslie Marmon. *Storyteller*. New York: Little, Brown, 1981.

Simon, Kate. *A Wider World*. New York: Harper & Row, 1986.

———. *Bronx Primitive*. New York: Harper & Row, 1982.

Smith, Sidonie. *A Poetics of Women's Autobiography*. Bloomington: Indiana University Press, 1987.

Spacks, Patricia Meyer. *Imagining a Self*. Cambridge, MA: Harvard University Press, 1976.

———. "Selves in Hiding." In *Women's Autobiography*, Estelle Jelinek, ed. Bloomington: University of Indiana Press, 1980, pp. 112–132.

Stanton, Domna C. *The Female Autograph: Theory and Practice of Autobiography from the Tenth to the Twentieth Century*. Chicago: University of Chicago Press, 1987.

———. "Books That Changed Our Lives." *Women's Studies Quarterly* 3–4 (1991): Introduction.

Steinem, Gloria. *Outrageous Acts and Everyday Rebellions*. New York: Holt, Rinehart & Winston, 1983.

Stevenson, Anne. *Bitter Fame: A Life of Sylvia Plath*. Boston: Houghton Mifflin, 1989.

Surrey, Janet L. "The Self-in-Relation: A Theory of Women's Development." In *Women's Growth in Connection: Writings from the Stone Center*, Judith Jordan et al., eds. New York: Guilford Press, 1991, pp. 51–66.

Swan, Brian, and Arnold Krupat. *I Tell You Now: Autobiographical Essays by Native American Writers*. Lincoln: University of Nebraska Press, 1987.

Truitt, Anne. *Daybook: The Journal of an Artist*. New York: Viking, 1982.

Theroux, Alexander. "Reading the Poverty of Rich." In *Reading Adrienne Rich: Reviews and Re-Visions, 1951–1981*, Jane Cooper, ed. Ann Arbor: University of Michigan Press, 1984, pp. 304–308.

Wades-Gayles, Gloria. *Pushed Back to Strength: A Black Woman's Journey Home.*
      Boston: Beacon Press, 1993.
Walker, Alice. *In Search of Our Mothers' Gardens.* New York: Harcourt Brace
      Jovanovich, 1983.
———. "Looking for Zora." In *Between Women,* Carol Ascher, Louise DeSalvo, and
      Sara Ruddick, eds. Boston: Beacon Press, 1984, pp. 431–449.
Wagner-Martin, Linda. *Sylvia Plath: A Biography.* New York: St. Martin's Press,
      1987.
Welty, Eudora. *The Collected Stories of Eudora Welty*: "Where Is the Voice Coming
      From?" (pp. 603–608), "A Worn Path" (pp. 142–153). New York: Harcourt
      Brace Jovanovich, 1980.
———. *One Writer's Beginnings.* Cambridge, MA: Harvard University Press, 1984.
Weintraub, Karl J. *The Value of the Individual: Self and Circumstance in Autobiogra-
      phy.* Chicago: University of Chicago Press, 1978.
Winnicott, D.W. *Playing and Reality.* London: Penguin, 1971.
Wolff, Sally. "Some Talk About Autobiography: An Interview With Eudora Welty."
      The Southern Review (Winter 1990): 80–88.
Wright, William. *Lillian Hellman, the Image, the Woman.* New York: Simon &
      Schuster, 1986.

◆ Index ◆

◆ About the Author ◆

Jeanne Braham received her Bachelor of Arts degree from the College of Wooster, her Master of Arts degree from the University of Pennsylvania, and her Doctor of Arts from Carnegie-Mellon University. She divides her time between teaching at Clark University and editing Heatherstone Press, a poetry publishing house specializing in hand-crafted poetry chapbooks. She has written essays on autobiography and memoir for The Georgia Review, Belles Lettres, and Modern Fiction Studies. Her book on the novels and short stories of Saul Bellow, *A Sort of Columbus*, was published by the University of Georgia Press. She has been awarded the Julian Ross Prize for Excellence in Teaching, an artist's fellowship in poetry at the Tyrone Guthrie Centre for the Fine Arts in Ireland, and a 1992–93 Associateship at the Five College Women's Studies Research Center at Mount Holyoke College.